GROWING UP
A FARM GIRL
SAVED MY
LIFE

Kirk House Publishers

GROWING UP
A FARM GIRL
SAVED MY
LIFE

A Cambodian Genocide Survivor Remembers

DONNA MAY SANDERS

Growing Up a Farm Girl Saved My Life:
A Cambodian Genocide Survivor Remembers ©
Copyright 2025 Donna May Sanders

First printing, August 2025
First edition

Paperback ISBN: 978-1-959681-94-6
eBook ISBN: 978-1-959681-96-0
Hardcover ISBN: 978-1-959681-95-3

Library of Congress Control Number: 2025912177

Published by Kirk House Publishers
1250 E 115th Street
Burnsville, MN 55337
612-781-2815

To order, visit: kirkhousepublishers.com
Quantity discounts are available.

TABLE OF CONTENTS

MAP

Provinces of Cambodia—map, webp—credit: Wikipedia

Veera on the farm in Sokmen's home village *Photo credit: Veera Som.*

VEERA SOM AND FAMILY MEMBERS

- My Mother: Ke Sang (Ke is last name)
- My Father: Som Por (Som last name, which he got from my grandpa)
- There were 11 siblings (including me). We were given my Grandpa Heang's last name. Years later, when we immigrated to America, my siblings and I took our father's last name, Som, as ours, which he had gotten from his grandpa, my Great Grandpa Som.
- My family members in birth order:
- First born. Heang Kim Sean, born in the Tiger Year, 1949. My sister Sean died from an illness when she was 13 years old.
- Second born. Heang Kim Yean, born in the Rabbit Year, 1950. My sister Yean died from starvation during the Khmer Rouge takeover at age 26.
- Third born. Heang Kim Yann, born in the Dragon Year, 1952. My sister Kim Yann died at two years of age.
- Fourth born. Me, (birth name) Heang Kim Yoeurn, born in the Horse Year, 10/9/1954 (also known as Veera Som)

- Fifth born. Heang Saroun, born in the Goat Year, 1955, died as a baby.
- Sixth born. Heang Sarem, born in the Monkey Year, 1957. Sudan and Sudon's mother died at age 42 of liver disease while in Cambodia.
- Seventh born. Heang Saly, born in the Pig Year, 1958.
- Eighth born. Heang Channy, born in the Cow Year, 1960
- Ninth born. Heang Navy, born in the Rabbit Year, 1963
- Tenth born. Heang Rithy, born in the Snake Year, 1965. My first brother, whose children were Mealea and Molly, died in Cambodia at age 32 from a car accident.
- Eleventh born. Heang Rithea, born in the Goat Year, 1968. My second brother

INTRODUCTION

I am a survivor of the Cambodian Genocide that took place under the Pol Pot regime between 1975 and 1979. My people lost everything that was familiar and ordinary. A communist group known as the Khmer Rouge stripped our country from us in a way that was unfathomable. Regardless of our economic status, whether very poor like me and my family or wealthy, the war devastated the lives of all Cambodian people. All of us were torn away from our homes, our villages, our cities, our families, and our religious practices. We were stripped of all possessions and material and monetary wealth. We were forced into a life of servitude to the Khmer Rouge, their leadership known as Angkar, who carried guns and killed indiscriminately, a total of between 1.5 and 2 million innocent men, women, and children during the Cambodian Genocide. They muzzled us with force and attempted every moment of every day to prevent us from using our voices, sharing our hearts with our loved ones, and exercising any personal freedoms.

Before I walk you through the dark days that my loved ones and I experienced during the Cambodian Genocide and the weeks, months, and years of my bondage, let me share with you the simple life that was mine in my youth before the Khmer

Rouge takeover. My family and I may have been poor peasant farmers, but we truly had all that we needed and more.

CHAPTER 1

GROWING UP IN CAMBODIA

Born October 9, 1954, to Som Por and Ke Sang, I was given the name Heang Kim Yoeurn at birth. My parents' fourth daughter, I was one of 11 siblings: nine daughters and two sons. I lost two sisters before I was nine. My parents were peasant farmers and rented land to farm that was located approximately 5 kilometers from our home. We lived in Thmey Village, Tamoueurn Subdistrict, in the countryside outside the city of Battambang in northwestern Cambodia.

Our house, built from bamboo, had a thatched roof made from sabovskia leaves. We had a dirt floor. Our only door was made of bamboo, and our one window was open to the elements and located at the back of the house. Our home was simply furnished. Dad built our family bed and our parents' bed from bamboo. The family bed was used both for sleeping and for eating our family meals. Mom made our pillows. She stuffed pillowcases with cotton from the trees and hand-stitched them together. A curtain divided our parents' bed from the children's bed.

We had a simple kitchen. Rocks were used as burners over a wood cooking fire. We had pots and pans, no indoor refrigeration, nor indoor plumbing. We ate rice at every meal, three times each day. Mornings we had plain rice soup for breakfast with dry baked fish. The children were in charge of cooking the rice. I began cooking rice when I was six years old. Lunch and dinner included fresh ingredients that we grew ourselves, primarily fruits and vegetables, with fish our primary source of protein. All of us caught the fish. The live catch was placed in a bamboo basket and immersed into the lake or river to keep the fish fresh until it was time to cook it. At mealtimes we clean, marinate, and cook fish. Sometimes we smoke it. Mud fish and catfish were commonplace. Tiny fish were pickled in jars. Mom taught us to cook, and we all pitched in preparing our meals, except for my father, who did not cook.

Bamboo shoots come from young bamboo trees. Our home was surrounded by bamboo trees. During the rainy season, bamboo shoots were plentiful and would be used as a main ingredient in soup. Both bamboo shoots and fish were easy to come by during the rainy season.

During the dry season, we ate more dried or smoked fish and vegetables. We raised lots of chicken and enjoyed eating chicken and eggs all year long. We cared for the chickens and threw rice at them each morning. We raised one or two pigs that were later sold for profit. We did not store food in the house, except maybe a few staples like salt, sugar, MSG (monosodium glutamate), and fish sauce. My mother made fish sauce. It could be stored in jars for many years. She also canned fish pickles (a.k.a. prahok), which had a long shelf life. There was no need for recipes for cooking. The same food was cooked every day and just got the "taste test." At mealtime, each of us got a rice bowl. When the stew or main dish was finished cooking, a bowl was set aside with portions for our mom and dad to share. They weren't usually home yet from working in the fields at mealtimes. My siblings and I sat in a circle on our bamboo bed, each with our rice bowl and spoon. We would then partake from the large serving bowl that was our family meal, which was placed in the center of the bed. The babies ate rice soup and softened bananas, as well as breast milk. In addition to farming, we grew fruit trees and vegetables, including bananas, mangoes, milk fruit trees, and pineapples. We also grew sugarcane and herbs.

Herbal remedies were used for medicinal purposes. We foraged for these leaves and roots. If one of us came down with a fever, we might be seen by a traditional Khmer Krou Khmer (an elderly traditional healer). Babies were born at home. An elderly woman served the village as a midwife and delivered us.

Our home had no running water. We did not have the machinery to dig a well. Rather, a pond was dug by hand and was located close to our home. The water from the pond was our family's drinking and bathing water. No sterilization was used before drinking it. Our family carried the water from the pond to our home daily with the aid of a shoulder board. We placed a bamboo pole across our shoulders and then hung a tin watering can on each end of the pole. We'd tip a little water out of one watering can to balance the other. We would also tip the watering cans from side to side to water rows of plants.

Cambodia has two seasons: the dry season from October through April (which is the harvest season) and the rainy season from May through September (a.k.a. the growing season). During the dry season, our pond would eventually dry up. This was a hardship. We would then have to walk farther to fetch the water, carrying it from the nearby lake or from the Thmey Canal.

We owned oxen to assist us with plowing the fields and had guard dogs as pets. The little money that we had was used to purchase necessities; medicine and staples like sugar, salt, and pork were purchased from the village market. The older children in our family didn't have opportunities to earn money to contribute to our family income.

Cows grazing in Cambodia. *Photo credit: Sokrey.*

We used gas lights inside our home. They were tin containers with a handle and resembled a watering can but without a spout. On top was a screw-on cap to fill with gasoline, which held a wick that was lit with a lighter. We used this light every night after dark. Our main mode of transportation was walking. We did have an old bicycle that I sometimes used to ride to and from school.

I suffered from asthma from an early age. In our culture, I was thought to be "hurt." I often had difficulty breathing and experienced shortness of breath. I sounded like a cat when I wheezed. Since my asthma made farming chores more difficult for me than for my siblings, my parents decided to send me to all twelve years of school, plus Terminal Class, unlike my siblings, who would only attend school through their primary years. My dad told my siblings not to be jealous of this privilege given to me because it was due only to my chronic asthma.

In Cambodia, our grade numbering system was reversed from American schools:

- Elementary School began with Grade 12 and went down through Grade 8
- Middle School: Grades 7, 6, 5 and 4; and
- High School: Grades 3, 2 and 1 and Terminal Class was the year of completion of school.

Schooling wasn't required for children in Cambodia. Children were enrolled in school at the discretion of their parents. Kids were assessed for readiness to begin school by raising their arm with their elbow up over their head. If the child's fingertips could reach the top of the ear on the opposite side of the head, they were enrolled; if not, the child was held back for another year. I was assessed for school readiness when I was seven years old, but my fingertips did not reach the top of my opposite ear, so I wasn't allowed to attend school until the following year after I turned eight.

Playtime

Kids playing holding hands. *Photo credit: Sokrey.*

The soil in our village was heavy with clay. In the dry season, when our pond would dry up, the other kids and I would slide down into the dry pond, riding on a bag or an old cloth. We molded little toys, including cows, dogs, little men, little women, and little children, out of damp clay we found below in the dry pond. These were our toys. We would fashion makeshift play-houses from twigs and sticks and play house with our handmade clay toys. Our playmates were our siblings and cousins. Swings were made from tree vines. We didn't have a playground, but we made our own. We were poor, but we had fun. We had plenty of food to eat and had peace of mind. We were happy.

Chores

We took turns with chores, washing the dishes and carrying the water. In the rainy season, we didn't have to carry the water as far. We were teased because we were farm kids. Farming was looked down upon in my culture.

My Education

Classroom and school children. *Photo credit: Sokrey.*

When I was eight years old, in 1962, I started school in Grade 12 in Thmey Village. (Grade 12 in Cambodia was the equivalent of Grade 1 in the US.) I wore a white blouse and a dark blue skirt. The boys wore a white button-down shirt and dark blue shorts. We walked to school. Sometimes one of us would ride our bike.

My siblings completed only the primary grades in school. Following completion of middle school, passing an entrance exam called the Diploma Test was required to advance to higher education. We had no books at home. There was nothing to read. There was no library in the village, nor at school, where I could borrow books. When a grocery item wrapped in the newspaper was brought home from the village, that newspaper was what I read. The only books I had to read were the schoolbooks that my parents purchased for me at extreme expense and sacrifice. My schoolbooks were invaluable to me.

From the age of twelve on up, Cambodian parents became increasingly strict with their daughters. We weren't allowed to go anywhere unchaperoned. Social activities were very limited. There was no movie theater in our village; however, movies were shown outdoors. This was a social gathering and required that mothers chaperone their daughters. Social gatherings took place at the temple. If parents didn't grant permission and a girl's mother did not chaperone her daughter, then the girl did not attend. I recall times, like most children, when I wanted permission to attend an event and my parents said no. I tried hard to persuade them by being very attentive to my chores beforehand. I'd take extra good care of the cow to earn my parents' favor. But my parents were extremely strict and weren't easily persuaded once they'd made up their minds. Sometimes Mom would say yes but

Dad would say no. Then I would cry. I had responsibilities that my parents always put first before pleasure. I had to get up at 5:00 a.m. each day to complete my homework and do chores before school. My parents prioritized my getting enough sleep ahead of socializing. We learned strict discipline.

My dad was a harsh disciplinarian and used the whip on us. He believed that if kids were physically punished for wrongdoing, it would be a deterrent from repeating the same behavior. Boys bullied me for caring for our cows. That was considered to be boys' work. My parents had nine daughters before they had their two sons. There was no choice but for the girls to care for the cow. To retaliate for the teasing once, I scooped out the meat of the mango fruit and threw it into the eye of the boy who taunted me. That was my way of standing up to a bully. The boy's mom brought her son to see my dad, showing him her son's inflamed eye. Rather than justifying my behavior and defending me, my father whipped me instead.

Even though Dad was harsh with his children, he was beloved by our family and others. He was a smart man, not educated, but wise. He was a peacemaker. He disciplined his children strongly as a way of teaching us right from wrong. He did not tolerate conflict.

Growing Rice

Green rice field. *Photo credit: Sokrey.*

Cambodians grew many varieties of rice, including jasmine and black rice. My father was a rice farmer.

My father planted 41.165 acres. He did not own the land that our family farmed. He rented it. We did own three plows, and each plow required two oxen apiece to operate. Our family owned a total of seven oxen in all.

Planting Rice

The Growing Season/also known as the Wet Season

May through September

Green rice field and canal. *Photo credit: Sokrey.*

When May arrives, the rice fields are still dry. My father, mother, and older sister would begin the work of plowing the field. Plowing was traditionally men's work, but because our parents' first nine children were girls, the girls had to do this work. The handheld plow was attached to one or two oxen. The plow had a heavy metal base, triangular in shape, that was guided by the farmer walking back and forth, going row by row to turn up the soil. This is exhausting work for both the oxen and the farmer. Frequent breaks were necessary, especially when working in sunny conditions.

Once the field was plowed, the rice that had been set aside the previous year for this year's planting was poured into large bamboo baskets. My father would take a basket and, on foot, walk the fields, throwing and spreading the rice over the plowed field. Dad preferred to spread the rice himself. By keeping the spreading/throwing motion consistent, he thought the rice would grow more uniformly.

Veera's Dad, Som Por, wearing krama. *Photo credit: Veera Som.*

Once the rice was spread, the rice fields were raked to cover the seed.

These steps completed the initial planting process. In Cambodia, from October through April, you can count on the sun, and now our family would await the much-needed rain to produce a bountiful crop.

My father did not plant our entire acreage all at once. Sometimes, he would plant a thicker crop in a separate area. He did this by spreading the seed very thick in the designated location. Three months later, during the rainy season, these rice plants would be pulled up and replanted. This practice was done to generate a superior rice crop. Because this process was labor-intensive, it was only done on a small scale.

Mom, my siblings, and I were also gardeners. We grew many vegetables, including cucumbers, mustard greens, lettuce, Asian squash, peppers, and eggplant. We also grew a variety of herbs, i.e., lemongrass and galangal (a root, like turmeric root). (*Note: I grew turmeric on my patio in Eagan. Turmeric derives from the ginger family and is used in cooking, as well as for medicinal purposes when dried and ground.*) Our garden in Thmey Village was strategically placed in front of our house and provided easy access for food preparation and cooking. The garden harvest was used to feed our family. Any surplus was sold at the village market.

I really loved growing flowers too. We grew many varieties along the outer edge of the vegetable garden in front of our home. My favorites were the ten o'clock flowers, sunflowers, marigolds, gypsy queen celosia, and jasmine. Lotus flowers were incredibly beautiful too and grew wild in the nearby lake. Sometimes we'd collect lotus flowers and deliver a pretty bouquet of them to the temple.

Lotus flower.
Photo Credit: Marina.

During the time between planting and harvesting, my father weaved baskets by hand from bamboo. Our family used them in our everyday life.

Straw basket Dad weaved. *Photo credit: Veera Som.*

The Harvest

The harvest season, also known as the dry season, extends from October through April

"When the rice paddies are golden, it's harvest time."

Golden rice field, ready for harvest. *Photo credit: Samphoun.*

At harvest time, my father, mother, siblings, and everyone available to help gather at the farm. All are needed for this labor-intensive process. In fact, my family and I move to the farm, living in a modest home alongside the rice field, for the entire harvest season, until the rice harvest is complete. There were times my father had to hire help to get the crop out before any rice paddies were lost.

Cutting Rice Paddies

We cut rice plants row by row by hand with a sickle. Being bent over like this for long days and months, working in the rice fields, is hard labor. Once we cut a large bunch, we secure it with a reed. These bunches are then piled up and later transported by ox cart to the threshing location. However, before rice paddies are ready for threshing, the rice plants are laid out to dry for two to three days.

Threshing

Threshing is the next step, the process to separate the grain (rice) from its plant. As peasant farmers, our father and family did everything by hand. In reflection, I feel warm with nostalgia in sharing just how we got things done. This is my heritage. Farming was our way of life. We farmed the land together. We prepared the ground for threshing by raking it smooth. Cow manure and water were then spread over the prepared ground and allowed to dry, creating a cementlike surface. Next, rice paddies were laid out in a circular pattern. Between four and seven oxen were then hooked up next to one another, and one of us would take the rope/rein and direct the oxen to walk in a circular motion around and around, stomping the rice paddies as they went, which in turn separated the rice from its straw plant. Occasionally, we would stop the oxen to inspect the status of the rice paddies and give the oxen a rest. While the oxen rested, we would use a changhe (a bamboo pole with a rounded hook) to turn the rice plants from bottom to top. After completing three rounds, the rice was separated from the rice paddies. The remaining plant was no longer a rice paddy but now it is just straw. We would then remove the straw from the separated rice, lifting the straw and shaking any remaining rice free.

After most of the straw was removed from the cementlike ground, we used a broom to sweep away any remaining dust from the rice itself. Once this process was completed, piles of rice were stacked. We would repeat this sequence over and over again until we had enough rice for the next step.

Cleaning the rice

We waited for a windy day to clean the rice (sift the rice from any small pieces of straw). A tool similar in shape to a shovel, but with a flat end, was used. We'd lift a batch of rice and toss it in the wind to sift the rice away from any remaining straw or straw dust. The sifted rice was then collected in a separate area close by. As you can imagine, this took a lot of time. We did this procedure for every piece of rice from the crop. Some farmers had a hand-cranking machine that the rice was poured into. A fan inside separates the straw dust from the rice.

Other times we paid to have it done by a machine. We owned a bamboo rice separator that we sometimes used for our family's rice supply only, as it processed the rice in small quantities. Once the rice was clean, it was distributed to 15-kilogram bamboo baskets. Any rice products deemed inferior to eat or sell were saved for feed for the chickens and pigs.

This completes the harvest.

Making Hay Mounds

My father taught us how to make hay mounds. We wrapped the straw around a bamboo pole, leaving the bamboo pole sticking out at the top. When completed, the stack is triangular in shape. The hay mounds are stored exactly where they are made. Dad taught us how to pull hay from these mounds in a way so as not to disturb the entire hay mound. As the hay mounds remained in place for a long time, and throughout the rainy season, mushrooms grew at their base. We harvested and ate those mushrooms. Nothing was left to waste.

Again, in the 1960s and 1970s when I grew up in Cambodia, the local peasant farmers performed all the steps of harvesting by hand. It was hard manual labor for my father, mother, my siblings, and me. It was backbreaking work, stooped over in the rice fields for hours, days, and months. Now, in the 21st century, Cambodian growers are renting farm machinery to accomplish their rice harvests. But back then we were extremely poor and didn't have the means to rent machinery to make our work easier.

Rice Storage
My father constructed a homemade silo to store the rice. The silo was made from bamboo and could be circular or rectangular in shape. Manure and water were used to waterproof it, a roof was built over it, and a shelter was built around it. When we transferred the rice from its storage silo, manufactured bags were used, having a capacity of 70 kilograms. These bags were made from the skin of a small tree called preal, also known as krochoa. Using these manufactured bags made for a uniform measurement for marketing and sales of rice.

Negotiating the Price of the Harvested Rice
Upon completion of the harvest, the landowner came to call on my parents. Again, my parents rented the land that we farmed. Landowners came to collect their share of the rice as payment for the rental of their land. Even though the cost of farmland rental was determined prior to the rice planting, my father and mother might attempt to renegotiate the price at this meeting, depending on whether it was a good or bad yield. My mom was the head of our household. She was a strong woman and negotiated with the

landowner on behalf of our family. My dad was a quiet man and spoke little. The rice crop was our currency (money) that would pay for necessities such as clothing, medication, health care costs, schoolbooks, and the like. Of course, we didn't exchange the rice for services or products but would rather sell the rice at the village market. These proceeds were our family's primary source of income. Fruit and vegetables from our garden supplemented our income. We sold rice at the village market and, in turn, collected money to purchase the products we needed. We were farmers. Our crop was our income. With the harvest complete and the rice in storage, our family relied on this year's harvest not only to provide the family's annual income but also because the rice was our staple food for the upcoming year. When there was a need to make purchases throughout the year, my mother sold the amount of rice necessary to exchange for currency for our family's purchases.

When the crop yield was large and plentiful, my parents, family, and I were very happy. But, when the harvest produced a poor yield because of poor growing weather conditions, this was cause for grave concern. This is when my mother would try to negotiate a reduced payment of rice with the landowner. We were already poor. A bad harvest could mean our family would not have enough food to eat in the coming year.

My Family Moves to the Jungle
In 1967, when I was 13 and in grade 7, my family experienced extreme poverty. My dad and mom had a poor harvest that year. We had no money and not enough food to eat. My dad walked

away from the rented farmland and moved our family to the Ampil Pram Daeum Village. This was a distant location where ample land was available to claim as our own. However, the land was located deep in the jungle. My parents worked extremely hard to clear a plot of land to farm in the jungle. It was a monumental task and very challenging to do by hand, but that is what we did. We dug the trees up and burned their roots. A great many wild animals lived in the jungle. There were wild pigs, elephants, deer, moose, tigers, and poisonous snakes, just to name a few. There was ample wood from the trees in the jungle. My dad built us a wooden house that stood high off the ground. Each night we burned firewood all night long to keep the wild animals at bay. I saw the milk of the tiger on the leaf of a tree but never saw the tiger. I never encountered an elephant either, but we heard their loud trumpet sounds echo throughout the jungle. There were many monkeys. We lived deep in the jungle. The trees were so old that you couldn't get your arms completely around their trunks.

During the initial summer months when my family moved to the jungle, I lived there with them. But, during the school year, my siblings and I who were in school, lived with my grandparents on my mother's side, since they lived closer to the school.

Farming in the Jungle

Once our family had cleared one or two meters of property (three to six feet, respectively), my parents began to plant. It wasn't possible to plow the cleared land because of its overall bumpy and rooted condition. Rather, we used a sharpened stick to poke the ground, then put the seeds down —all completed by hand. It was ridiculously arduous work. We planted corn, soybeans, and vegetables. After about one year's time, we had enough land cleared so my dad was able to begin planting rice.

While my parents and family worked on the land, we'd encounter jungle natives who were hunters. These men and boys wore no shirts or shoes, and their wild native appearance made me uneasy. I'd hide when I saw them approaching. I would spot them with their bloodied prey slung over their bare backs as they made their way back to their jungle homes. The jungle natives were not knowledgeable about money. They would trade their meat in the village for staples.

While we were working on the land, I saw poisonous snakes that were big, fat, and exceptionally long. My dad never killed them. We just chased them away. These were dangerous living conditions. Our cows stayed under our house for safekeeping. Because we built fires every night to keep the wild animals away, we trusted our cows were safe.

Mom Survives Oxcart Accident

Water resources were sparse. Small streams ran through the jungle but only during the rainy season. We hauled our water from the jungle stream and always boiled it before using it. During the dry season, we had to travel to a faraway village by oxcart for our water supply. The land was incredibly rough, gnarly, and bumpy. There were no roads in the jungle. When we were able, we'd reuse the tracks left by oxcarts that traveled before us. One day my mom was traveling some distance by oxcart to haul water. The terrain was bumpy and gnarly. A large container of water was perched atop the oxcart, and my mom was seated next to it. The oxcart tipped over. My mother was not seriously harmed in the accident but did receive injuries that took time to recover from. Life was challenging.

Our Successful Jungle Harvest

After one and a half years of my parents' and siblings' diligence in working the jungle land, we were overjoyed to achieve a successful harvest of rice, soybeans, corn, hot peppers, and the like. We also had kabass (a cotton plant). We hauled our harvest back to our village market to sell, and we did well. My parents had persevered through significant adversity and succeeded. This was a time of celebration.

Following the harvest, it was common to take a one- to two-hour break each day in the afternoon, but not our dad, he didn't take breaks. Instead, he took us further into the jungle to dig and cut bamboo shoots that were plentiful there. The only problem was that the bamboo shoots were heavy and difficult to carry back home. As I've said, there were no roads. The jungle floor presented so many impediments to walking, like vines, trees, and roots to navigate. It was a densely wooded jungle. Once, even though we hadn't traveled far, we got lost because the vegetation was so thick and low hanging that we couldn't find our way home. Dad ended up climbing a tree to gain a broader view of which direction to go. We had no compass for navigation. In the late afternoon, we would touch the side of a tree, and if it was warm, it indicated west. You don't want to be lost in the jungle at sunset. We started hearing the calls of wild jungle animals. The trumpet sound of the elephants, P-A-W-O-O, echoed throughout the jungle. Once our dad got us back on track and we knew which way to go, we still had to haul the bamboo shoots we'd bagged and that were slung over our shoulders. They were heavy and made our walking difficult and slow, but we made it home without any wild animal encounters.

Once home, we cleaned and boiled the bamboo shoots. Next, we sliced them up and dried them out. Once this was accomplished, we'd take a load to market to sell. Bamboo shoots were a popular ingredient in broths, so they were very marketable.

Illness and Loss

Unexpectedly, tragedy hit our extended family living nearby in the jungle. My first cousins, a boy and a girl, contracted a fever. Both went into comas and died quickly. We didn't understand what was causing these devastating losses. Folklore passed along to us by the local fortuneteller and the Krou Khmer (the local herbalist) was that my family and our relatives, by coming to the jungle and taking property without permission, were suffering the consequences of those actions. One week later, my uncle-in-law passed away in just the same manner. The fortuneteller was consulted and predicted more family members would experience the same fate.

Leaving the Jungle

That was it. Our family and extended relatives left behind all we had accomplished in the jungle that year and moved back to Thmey Village. I was 15 years old and was skeptical of the advice from the fortuneteller and the Krou Khmer. Years later, after studying medicine in school, I learned about the disease malaria. I believe now that it was cerebral malaria that took their lives. Had we been living in the village at that time, there was malaria medicine available that could have saved their lives.

Mom Sick with Hepatitis B

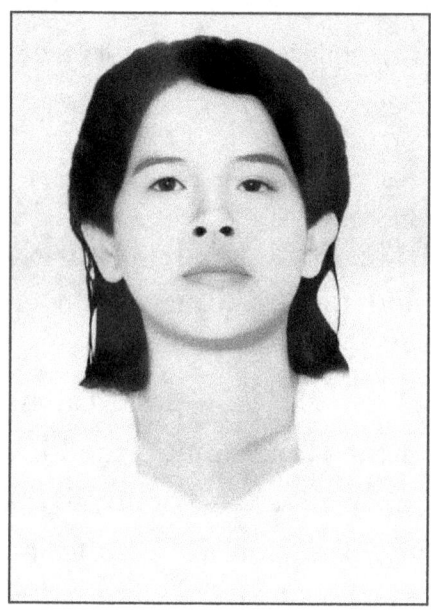

Mom, Ke Sang, her only photo. *Photo credit: Veera Som.*

My mother was just 39 years old when we returned to Thmey Village. By then she'd been the mother of 11 children (having already lost three of her children: her first-born, Heang Kim Sean, died at age 13; her third-born, Heang Kim Yann, died at age 2; and her fifth-born, Heang Saroun, died when she was a baby). Mom was recuperating from her oxcart accident and was suffering from a painful distended belly. Knowing nothing about the cause of my mother's affliction, there were villagers who believed that she was cursed. Others suspected that she was pregnant. Neither were right. Mom was suffering from the fatal stage of untreated Hepatitis B called ascites. However, at that time neither my mom nor our family understood anything about her condition. I accompanied my mother to her doctor appointments. We understood her condition was life-threatening and were desperately looking to the medical professionals for answers but we were only provided with rudimentary information: Mom had fluid in her belly; they would do a procedure to remove the fluid from her abdomen to relieve pressure on her other organs and allow her to breathe more freely and comfortably; a diuretic was prescribed, and she was sent home. Mom also saw the herbal medicine doctor, who prescribed herbal remedies. All we understood from her doctor was that Mom would not survive.

Developing a Strong Desire for a Future Career in Health Care

It was then that I developed a strong desire to become a healthcare professional so that I could someday offer patients and their loved ones more informed and compassionate care. In retrospect I understand that my mother was in the final and fatal stage of Chronic Hepatitis B. Chronic Hepatitis B, if left untreated, can progress to cirrhosis of the liver, where healthy liver tissue is replaced by scar tissue and inflammation of the liver can occur. If cirrhosis goes untreated, ascites, the accumulation of fluid in the abdominal cavity can occur which is common in patients with cirrhosis. Because my mother's liver disease progressed to ascites before diagnosis and treatment of Hepatitis B, the village doctor told us there was little that could be done to treat her.

My Family Starting Over

So now Mom and Dad had to start over. Dad resumed renting the same farmland that he had farmed previously. In addition, he began building a new house located closer to the road. Our family resumed our previous farming routine.

Furthering My Education — The Diploma Test

This was a chaotic time for our family. We had just returned to Thmey Village from the jungle. Dad was busy building the new house. Mom was doctoring for liver disease. My parents had small children who needed to be cared for, and we had farming and gardening to resume. There were many commitments for my time. I helped my mother with the kids, with household chores, raising the pigs, chickens, and gardening. Kim Yean, my older sister, spent most of her time working on the farm with Dad. I had very little time for my studies, and little resources, like study materials to advance my learning from home.

When I was 18 years old, during the final months of my middle school years, I took the Diploma Test. I cannot overstate how important passing the Diploma Test was to me. Not only was a passing grade needed to move on to high school, but successfully passing the Diploma Test allowed for advancement to potential teaching jobs and other careers. I failed the test, and I was devastated. Because I was humiliated that I'd failed the exam, I did not want to remain in school. I begged my parents to let me quit school, but they refused. I pleaded with them not to force me to return to the school where I'd failed the Diploma Test. After much consideration, my parents decided to send me to Siem Reap, a nearby province, to study and then retake the exam. Arrangements were made for me to stay with my uncle Chhorn and his wife who lived in Siem Riep. My mother had cared for Chhorn like a mother from an early age, after their mother had died.

Moving to Siem Reap Province to Study

I relocated to Siem Reap, moved in with my uncle and auntie-in-law, and began studying earnestly to retake the Diploma Test. This was an intensely challenging time. My mother was very sick back home, and I had just failed an exam that was critically important to me. My Uncle Chhorn was financially stable, not poor like my family. While living in his home, I began to resent my uncle for not financially supporting my mother throughout her health crisis. Soon, I became morose and depressed. My uncle and auntie-in-law did not speak with me. Food was placed on the table for me, and then I ate my meals alone. I had no one to talk to. My uncle was a quiet man. My auntie-in-law had her two sisters living with us. They weren't friendly to me. I felt unwelcome. The sisters knew the Cambodian language, but instead spoke only Vietnamese in my presence, a language that I didn't understand. I felt like they were speaking badly about me, in my presence.

My Mother Deathly Ill

Here I was far away from home, studying for this important exam, and I was miserable. This was my circumstance for nine months. Then I received a letter delivered to me by taxi, summoning me to return home. My mother had slipped into a coma. It was customary in my culture that a young woman be chaperoned wherever she went. I asked my uncle to accompany me home immediately. Uncle Chhorn said it would have to wait. I didn't understand that. My mom was his sister. She cared for him like a mother when he was young. Now she was gravely ill. I could not wait. I decided to go alone. I rode my bicycle to school to notify my teacher. I was given permission to be absent from school for one week to visit my sick mother.

I traveled alone by taxi. Once the taxi arrived at my parents' door I ran inside. Nobody was there. I was frightened and screamed, *"Where is my mother?"* The neighbor told me that Mom was gravely ill and that she was carried to my uncle's house, about one-half kilometer from home. Sobbing, I ran to my uncle's house. When I arrived, I found many people surrounding Mom as she lay flat on the bamboo bed. I made my way through the people encircling her and got in close to her. I caressed her skin, hugged her, and assured Mom that I was there with her. I begged of her, *"Please Mom, open your eyes."* She was not able. She was comatose. My mother passed away the next day, Wednesday, April 12, 1972.

Metal gong at temple. *Photo credit: Venerable Vichit Chum.*

In Cambodian tradition, an elder clanged a metal gong. (The gong was borrowed from the temple and had already been delivered to my uncle's home in anticipation of her death.) This metal gong signified to the villagers that one of them had passed away. Once the notification by gong was received, people came immediately to my uncle's house to pay their respects and assist our family with funeral preparations. Some brought wood to build a casket. Others brought food: meat, vegetables, and rice. Some went to the temple to borrow pots and pans, bowls, and utensils to serve the funeral guests who would soon be gathering.

I so value the Cambodian custom that when family is thrust deep into mourning, the community of extended family, friends, and neighbors come together and provide for and serve the funeral guests. The family doesn't have to do it. Our father was the person to direct what needed to be done, and the others just did it. He encouraged his children to: *"Stop your crying and welcome our guests."* My Uncle Chhorn, who I'd been living with, arrived after my mom passed away. He remained for the funeral.

My Mother's Traditional Cambodian Funeral

Historic home-village wat (temple) where Veera's parents' human remains are. *Photo credit: Samphoun.*

Gate of historic home village wat (temple). *Photo credit: Samphoun.*

The following day, Thursday, April 13, 1972, Mother's funeral ceremony began. It coincided with the Cambodian New Year. Many activities of celebration were scheduled for the Cambodian New Year at the temple. It was heartwarming to our family that many who planned to attend those celebrations chose to join us in mourning instead.

In keeping with our culture, the deceased mother's children gathered around her, washed her feet, and then requested forgiveness of her for any transgressions that we may have committed. Afterward, my mother, wearing her dress clothes, was placed in her coffin and it was closed. Each day people came to pay their respects. The monks were present every day from 10:30 a.m. until noon to chant. The monks returned each evening to resume chanting. A speaker was placed in a nearby tree, and funeral music was played throughout the day. This went on for two or three days. We waited for all my mother's siblings to arrive to pay their respects.

Pallbearers carried Mother in a funeral procession to the land where she raised our family. Our father; my siblings and me; her siblings, their families; friends; and neighbors all walked along in this procession. Once we arrived at our destination, her casket was placed on a platform. Everybody gathered there, and the monks chanted for the final time at the public funeral. The funeral ceremony ended. Our guests left. Once the family were the only ones remaining, the casket was opened to allow the family to view our mother's face one last time.

My family left then, and officials performed the cremation. Following the cremation, we returned to the site to collect our mother's remains. We gathered them, placed them in an urn, and carried them home. The next morning the monks came to our home and chanted one last time. The funeral ended on the third day.

Following my mother's funeral, I went back to Siem Reap to live with my Uncle Chhorn and auntie-in-law. I was extremely stressed. I had just lost my mom and I was concerned about the welfare of my four-year-old little brother. I was very uncomfortable living at my uncle's home. My relationship with my auntie-in-law and her two sisters was strained. I worried a lot about retaking the Diploma Test in just three months. It was a dark time for me, and I couldn't think clearly. According to my auntie everything I did to contribute to the household chores, I did wrong. I felt more like a servant in the household than family. I cried daily and worried constantly about the upcoming Diploma Test. I felt desperate and had lost hope for better days ahead.

Losing Hope, Desperately Seeking an Escape

One day I decided the answer to my problems was to take my own life. I collected many pills and held them in my hand. I was ready to swallow them to end my misery. But then I had a vision. My youngest brother Rithy was calling to me: *"Sister! When will you come back? I miss you!"* In that moment, I paused. *"Who will take care of my family if I kill myself and am no longer here?"* I thought about how hard my parents had worked to afford to send me to school to complete my education. Then I changed my mind. I would not take my life. I returned the pills to their original place.

Exercising My Independence, Choosing a Peaceful Study Place

That same day, I decided to run away. I packed up my clothes and books, piled them on the back of my bicycle, and left. I rode to my Uncle Thoeury's house (Uncle Chhorn's brother) and asked to stay there for three months to live and study for the Diploma Test. I admitted to him how miserable I'd been at Uncle Chhorn's. In the meantime, Uncle Chhorn returned home from work and discovered that I had left. He heard that I was at his brother Thoeury's and sent someone there to bring me back. I returned to Uncle Chhorn's home, apologized for leaving without discussing it with him first, but insisted that I could not live there any longer because I felt unwelcome by his wife and her two sisters. Uncle Chhorn gave me advice: *"You know that when you live together that you must be patient. It's like when you have more than* one bowl in the same basket. The bowls may collide and hit each other. If you're not careful, the bowls might break." So, uncle advised, "Veera, you must be patient." I listened to my uncle's advice and then responded, "Uncle, my patience has hit its limit. If I stay here as you ask, in the same basket, my bowl will surely break." Then I moved in with Uncle Thoeury. It was a far better place for me to study.

CHAPTER 2

CAMBODIAN GENOCIDE

Led by Pol Pot and the Communist Khmer Rouge

King Norodom Sihanouk ruled Cambodia from 1953 to 1970, first as a monarch then becoming its constitutional leader after Cambodia gained independence from France in 1953. He tried to remain neutral during the Vietnam War but faced increasing opposition during that time. Sihanouk was overthrown by Lon Nol in 1970 in a United States-backed coup. Lon Nol, the Cambodian Prime Minister, established the pro-American Khmer Republic. Lon Nol's government fought a brutal civil war against the communist Khmer Rouge. In spite of US military aid and bombings against the Khmer Rouge, Lon Nol's army struggled to control the countryside. After Sihanouk was overthrown in 1970, he aligned himself with the communist Khmer Rouge, led by Pol Pot, who were actively fighting against Lon Nol's government. This fight was the Cambodian Civil War. Sihanouk's support of the Khmer Rouge offered the Khmer Rouge legitimacy and popular appeal. However, Pol Pot's ideology was extreme and was using Sihanouk as a figurehead to gain support for the Khmer Rouge.

~Historical Reference as told to me by Sokmen Yem

In the Early 1970s, the Khmer Rouge Army, Their Leadership Known as "Angkar," Grew Their Army in the Jungle by Force
Fighting was taking place on the outskirts of Battambang. High School Siem Reap, where I attended school, was forced to close its doors because of the Khmer Rouge presence in the area. We, the students at High School Siem Reap, had to transfer to Middle School Angkor (College Angkor) to continue with our studies. It was three months later that I passed the Diploma Test. The obstacles and challenges I faced in successfully passing the Diploma Test had been formidable. I was very happy and relieved to successfully achieve this goal, and to make my family proud.

I had reached a crossroads in determining the future direction of my life. I had already been given opportunities that were unique to me in my family, those of furthering my education—because the conditions on the farm were challenging for my health given my asthma. My older sister, Kim Yean, representing my deceased mother, offered two options for me to move forward. 1) I could return home to Thmey Village and resume a life of farming; or 2) I could relocate to Battambang to continue my education. It was clear to me. I wished to relocate to Battambang to continue my education. In 1973 a female classmate of mine from Thmey Village and I relocated to Battambang and moved into a home that was owned by my uncle Ke Seng (my mother's brother). I completed second grade (grade 11).

One year later, in 1974, while I was attending first grade (grade 12), there were many protests taking place in the streets around the market in Battambang. I understood the protests to be largely by students to draw attention to the prohibitive costs for student rent, food, and retail. Protestors were seeking to have limits imposed on business owners for their goods and services.

At the end of this school year, I successfully passed the Baccalaureate 1 Test. Again, this was a major achievement for me. I was the first in my family to ever make it this far in school. The Baccalaureate 1 Test was the entrance exam for my final year of school known as "Terminal Class."

1975 — Terminal Class

I began Terminal Class in 1975. Terminal Class organized its students into three groups based on each student's baccalaureate test scores in the areas of science, math, and literature. I was enrolled in the Khmer Literature Program. Historically, Cambodia had been colonized by France. French literature was taught in the schools. In 1953 Cambodia became independent of France, yet in the 1970s when I was a student, French Literature remained the literature offering.

My Terminal Class studies ended abruptly.

Khmer Rouge – Its Leadership, Angkar

Khmer Rouge troops had been building their army in the jungle. At night, their leadership group, calling themselves "Angkar," ransacked homes in the villages located on the outskirts of the city. Angkar used force to recruit parents and children to go with them to the jungle to be trained as Khmer Rouge soldiers. They confiscated their personal property. Those who resisted were killed. The lawless of the land were volunteering for the Khmer Rouge army, and the Khmer Rouge grew strong. Many fled their homes in advance of anticipated raids. My siblings escaped to Battambang. Kim Yean, my elder sister, brought my younger siblings to live with me and my roommate in Battambang. She carried with her as much food as she could. My father stayed behind at home to continue to farm. He believed that left alone, in the event of the Khmer Rouge troops invading his property, that he could hide. He remained at home to continue to farm to provide for his family. My father had lots of chickens and cows that needed to be fed and rice fields to tend to. We worried about our father's safety at home. We knew that there was much fighting occurring overnight.

By April 1975, the Khmer Rouge had overthrown Lon Nol's army. Norodom Sihanouk initially became head of state but was quickly sidelined by the Pol Pot regime and placed under house arrest. The Cambodian Genocide took place under Pol Pot's leadership. Pol Pot was the leader of the communist Khmer Rouge and served as the prime minister of Democratic Kampuchea from 1975 to 1979. During this time, the Khmer Rouge carried out mass executions, forced labor, and starvation policies that led to the death of an estimated 1.5 to 2 million people.

~Historical Reference [as told to me by Sokmen Yem]

Khmer Rouge Takeover

On April 17, 1975, the Khmer Rouge army descended on Battambang, where I lived. The army, dressed in black, arrived with tanks. I remember them waving their white flags and claiming, *"We're here in peace."* President Lon Nol was officially ousted and had fled Cambodia just days before. The Khmer Rouge seized power. Norodom Sihanouk was installed initially as the head of state to maintain an appearance to the people of the Khmer

Rouge's legitimacy. However, Pol Pot was the actual leader of the Khmer Rouge regime. We as citizens were told by the Khmer Rouge that we would finally live in peace. There would be no more fighting. We wanted to believe that.

The citizens welcomed the Khmer Rouge army at first and were happy. Everyone was tired of all the fighting and the unrest. The citizens wished to believe what the Khmer Rouge said was true, that peace had finally come. So, for a few days, citizens were hopeful. I was too. Many families who had previously fled to the city returned to their family homes and villages, including my siblings. People were eager to resume their normal lives and get back to work. I remained in Battambang believing that I would resume my education and complete Terminal Class.

Cambodian Genocide

Before long, the Khmer Rouge, using megaphones in the streets, announced that Lon Nol's army, the Khmer Republic soldiers, were invited to attend a meeting. All the republican soldiers were told to wear their uniforms, including their badges depicting their rank. My neighbor, an air force pilot, husband, and father, did as instructed and dressed in his uniform and left for the meeting. His wife waited and waited for her husband to return. Later, while I was outside visiting with his wife and other neighbors, a man we knew arrived on his motorcycle. He told us that he had just been to Phom Sompov Village, and he was upset. He recounted witnessing large troops of uniformed officers unloaded from a truck who were then executed right there on the farm before his eyes. He reported that *"The Khmer Rouge soldiers shot all of them, laid them out on the ground, then using a dirt mover covered them over with dirt."* He warned all to be extremely careful, telling us that if called to attend a meeting not to attend. The Khmer Rouge were systematically gathering like groups of people in positions of authority, power, and intellect: first were the soldiers; then came the police, medical doctors, lawyers, professors. Those educated and perceived to be powerful were called to meetings and then executed. Lastly, the Khmer Rouge called on the students to attend a meeting. My roommate and I did not go to the meeting. This was how the genocide in my country of Cambodia began.

Prior to the *"students'"* meeting announcement, we were told not to attend school because the Khmer Rouge had to clean the schools and the city. My uncle Ke Seng, my mother's brother whose house we were living in, worked for border security. A photo of him in uniform hung on our wall. After hearing about the killings, I immediately removed his photo from the wall, gathered up his unloaded gun kept in our home, and buried it outside. Had the Khmer Rouge soldiers seen these things when they inspected our home, we would have been killed.

Mass Evacuation. Cleaning the City

Next, the Khmer Rouge soldiers went up and down the streets of Battambang, announcing by megaphone that King Sihanouk wanted to clean the city of Battambang. All residents were ordered to leave their homes immediately. My roommate and I were at home. We watched the soldiers arriving on our street. We met them outside where they pointed their guns at us and told us to leave immediately. We had heard that they were coming.

We quickly ran back into the house. I grabbed my philosophy book. It was expensive, and I believed I'd be returning to finish my education. Then we packed some food: rice, dry fish, and a bottle of water. Lastly, we packed some clothes. Kim Chhay, my roommate; my neighbor; and I then left our homes. The street was full of people. The soldiers told us to walk south, but my family home was north in Thmey Village. Since the streets were so crowded, my roommate and I were able to easily mix in with the crowd walking north instead.

Walking along the road, I didn't dwell on my worries as I witnessed the plight of others around me. A neighbor of mine carried his elderly mother on his back, so was unable to carry any provisions with them. Crying was heard all around us. A few hours later, everybody was questioning, *"Where are we going?"* Because I was walking in the direction of my family home, I had hope. I anticipated meeting up with my family. That's what kept me motivated to continue walking mile after mile. We walked 30 kilometers (18 miles) that first day. Families: men, women, and children, some crying, others sick, we kept our sorrows and fears to ourselves as we observed the Khmer Rouge soldiers pointing their guns our way.

Khmer Rouge soldiers. *Photo credit: Documentation Center of Cambodia Archives.*

My siblings were on the lookout for me and spotted me as we arrived in Thmey Village at sunset. Angkar told us we could stay with nearby villagers overnight if they had a place for us. Many found rest that night roadside. I was relieved to see that my father and siblings had not yet been evacuated. My roommate and I stayed the night in my family home. My family all looked so sad. My father inspected the items that I had carried with me on my back and saw the few books I carried with me. Immediately he became very frightened and agitated. He whispered quietly to me, *"This is not peace. You will not be going back to school in Battambang."* He continued that he had seen many dead soldiers fallen on our farm. Father urged me, *"Please be careful"* and gave me this advice: *"Daughter, please do not tell them that you're a student."* He said that he'd heard the Khmer Rouge were killing everybody they learned could read and write, as well as those who were wealthy. He implored me, *"Never admit to being a student."* My father shed tears as he spoke. I had never seen my father cry, not even when my mother died. I knew what a dire situation we were in, and I feared what would come next. Father didn't believe that all of us would be able to remain together in our home. In anticipation of evacuation, he began gathering food, clothing, and necessities for us to transport by oxcart. Then my father, using his children as lookouts for the Khmer Rouge, took my schoolbooks from my backpack and hastily buried them out in the field. I was so frightened and sad. We all felt such hopelessness.

A few years prior, when I lived and went to school in Siem Reap, I was best of friends with my neighbor, Vanney Kloc. Her father was wealthy. They owned a big house. They had been kind to me. Sometime later, Vanney was sent to study at the Pharmacy School in Phnom Penn. Today, during the tumult in the streets, Vanney appeared in front of my home. Her grandmother and cousin Mouy were with her. They were happy to see me and asked if they could stay the night with us in my father's home. We welcomed them and were happy to have them.

The next morning the Khmer Rouge announced that everybody was to evacuate their homes immediately. Everyone would go to work in the fields. The Khmer Rouge intended to implement their plan to transform Cambodia into a one-class agrarian society that would serve the Khmer Rouge. They were determined to identify all non-farmers as "the enemy" and kill them. The Khmer Rouge army, both boy and girl soldiers, knocked on the doors of all the homes in Thmey Village and, with guns drawn, ordered everybody to evacuate immediately. If a household had prepared supplies in advance to take along, they were allowed to carry those things with them, either by hand or by oxcart. If nothing was prepared, the soldiers forced people to leave with nothing.

My father had been preparing for our departure and was ready. We took two cows and an oxcart to carry our family's belongings. The oxcart was piled with pots and pans, dishes, and food items, including rice, dried fish, fish pickles, vegetables, salt, and sugar. The pigs and chicken we left behind. Each of us carried a bundle of our clothing as we walked. The street was full of people. Various soldiers led groups in different directions. Our family was directed to walk west. We were given no further explanation as to where our destination would be. We were required to walk in a single file. Soldiers kept order from the side of the road with their guns drawn. We walked 16 km to the next village. My family, friends, and the rest of our large group were later led off the road and onto a farm. Other groups continued in various directions, with different leaders.

Khmer Rouge Work Camps

The Khmer Rouge announced that our group would be staying at this location. On the first night on this farm together, my siblings and I all slept beneath our oxcart. My friend, her grandmother, and her cousin remained with us. We ate food left over from morning and then slept. Others cooked their food there. Soon everybody was asleep.

The next morning everybody received orders to gather the materials needed to build individual shelters. We gathered bamboo, leaves, plastic bags, and anything that could be used to erect a shelter and provide protection from the elements. The nearby village had already been evacuated. We were allowed to pillage these village homes for food and the materials to make our shelters. Building our shelters for what was to be our first work camp took two or three days.

Angkar Begins Indoctrinating Its Workers

Angkar, the Khmer Rouge leadership, called a *"Bohn"* (campwide brainwashing meeting). They laid out the Khmer Rouge goals, saying, *"You know when you learned the theory of everything in school, but never practiced it? Now, the time has come to practice it."* We were told there would no longer be any schools, no more government officers, nor anybody in positions of authority. All Cambodian people would now be farmers. We would plant all the land. Our meeting took place under a shade tree. There would no longer be rich people, nor poor people. Nobody would be allowed to keep any personal possessions. Going forward, our individual belongings would consist of one bowl and one spoon. Individual family units would no longer exist. Everybody would become our siblings. We were no longer to have any allegiance to our parents. Nobody will. Our allegiance would be to Angkar, and only Angkar. Women and girls must wear our hair short. From now on, everybody was to wear only black.

Following the meeting, the girls got their hair cut in bobs and we dyed our clothing as black as possible. We collected branches from a tree and then boiled them. The liquid produced by this process was quite dark. We soaked our clothing in this mixture and then dumped our clothing in the mud and stomped on them to darken them further. Afterward, we washed our dingy clothing. Sometimes the result was more of a dark gray than black, but this was acceptable to Angkar.

Angkar moved from shelter to shelter, taking the census of each shelter: its number of inhabitants, our names, ages, and sex. I changed my name at this time to Kim Soeurth. Angkar confiscated any food families had in their possession, as well as any personal artifacts. Angkar stripped us of all personal belongings. My sister Channy had heard what Angkar was doing before they arrived at our shelter. Channy didn't want us to give up the meager provisions that we had on hand. She poured some of our rice into a bag, flattened the bag as best she could, and slipped it under the floor mat to hide it. When Angkar arrived, I was so afraid of what the consequences might be for hiding rice that I removed the rice from under the mat and relinquished it to Angkar. My sisters Channy and Heang Sarem were so mad at me for doing that. They were young and still naïve as to what their actions might cost them.

Once the census was completed for the population of our camp, another meeting was convened. Now Angkar had the breakdown of everybody living in camp. Leadership began separating our camp into groups of similar ages. They began with girls between the ages of 15 and 20 years. My name was called. I was instructed to line up with the group of girls my age. The boys in this age group were also separated out at this time. Within our age group, we were divided into smaller groups. No siblings were allowed to remain together. Children ten years of age and younger would remain with their parents. We were instructed to return to our shelters, pick up one bowl, one spoon, and some clothing, and return to our newly assigned groups immediately.

Once we had reconvened into our groups, we were divided into smaller groups of ten people. One person from each group of ten was selected to be a group leader (Krom leader). Next, each group of ten was divided by three pouks. A pouk leader (section leader) was assigned for each group of three.

Now that our work groups had been assigned, my group left our home camp. We walked two or three kilometers, then set up a temporary camp. My age group's team of 15- to 20-year-olds became what were known as "Korng Chalatt" (nomads) that moved from place to place to work. We had no home base for sleeping. We slept in any sort of shelter found near the fields we were working in. We became working nomads and on the move all the time. I made a hammock from a sack used for rice and slept hanging from a tree limb. At 20, I weighed just 88 lbs. (My weight dropped to 75 lbs. as the years under the Khmer Rouge passed by.) I had no toothbrush, no soap nor shampoo, nothing really, but I may have had an old comb with me. My modest luxury item.

Dam construction Communist Khmer Rouge Work Camp. *Photo credit: Documentation Center of Cambodia Archives.*

Our female Korng Chalatt's first job was to dig a canal for directing rainwater to flow to the farmland. We were provided digging implements: shovels and hoes. We would work, work, work. Sometimes we wore hats for protection from the hot sun. Other times we did not. It was hard, manual labor. Our group leaders were responsible for seeing that we did our work well and that we completed our assigned tasks. Daily meetings were held with the full camp. Job-related information was discussed, and we were repeatedly counseled about Angkar's values. We were constantly reminded that Angkar is to always come first. Angkar liked to preach, *"In our old lives the poor were looked down upon, but not anymore, everybody is now equal."* Now we were all poor, with no possessions and no personal freedoms at all.

Angkar was forever directing us to report anyone who was not performing well or who spoke negatively about Angkar. We quickly learned that it was best not to trust anybody.

People from our group were selected to cook for the camp. The cooks delivered our meals to the field. Our individual bowl and spoon were always kept with us. We received soup with just a bit of rice, water grass, and salt. That was it. There was no substance to the soup at all. This was the sustenance we were given to work long, hard days in the field. We were given five minutes to eat. We worked from sunrise to sunset. Oftentimes, lights were set up in the field and we'd be required to work well beyond sunset.

Khmer Rouge Public Killings of *"The Enemy"*

In September 1975 (rainy season), our team's assignment was to assist the Elder Group in the Sahakor located in the village of Kean Kess. Our team slept in the village temple. The first time that I stepped inside the wat (temple), tears flowed down my face. The temple was empty and eerily quiet, absent of the Buddhist monks. The temple had been our place of worship, where respect and gratitude were paid to Buddha. Now the girls' team was using the temple as a place to sleep, inside the Preh Vihear (the monks' sleeping quarters). The monks had been forcibly removed by the Khmer Rouge, forced to remove their orange robes and join the workers in the field. The Khmer Rouge forbids religion. I knew the temple as a place where monks were present, wearing their orange robes; ceremonies took place where people dressed up in traditional clothing. The temples were decorated with beautiful flowers, where the sounds of the monks chanting to Buddha could be heard morning and night. The temple was a welcoming place where we came to listen to the monks' wise advice and hear their chanting. Now the monks were nowhere to be found. The Buddha statues had been destroyed. My heart was broken, but I could only acknowledge this inwardly. The Khmer Rouge forbid any allegiance to anyone or anything, except Angkar.

One day during this period of time, while staying at the temple and planting the rice field, I heard the sound of a whistle. All the workers of the Korng Chalatt teams, both male and female, were instructed to stop our work immediately. We were summoned to attend a meeting in the Kean Kess Temple. I wondered what could be so urgent that Angkar would call a meeting in the middle of the day while we were all busy at work? Upon arriving inside the temple, I saw the elders' team, the men's team, and the girls' team all assembling on the floor in a wide circle adjacent to the Preh Vihear, the side building where the girls' team slept. One soldier was carrying his gun and standing in the center of the circle. The Angkar chief began to speak: *"Do you know why we are bringing you all together here for a meeting?"* Nobody uttered a word. Angkar continued, *"We want to show you the enemy that we just captured."* I turned my gaze away from the center of the circle and saw two soldiers directing a man and a woman whose hands were bound behind their backs into the center of the circle. *Also present at the meeting were* additional soldiers off to the side, as well as the family of the man escorted into the center of the circle (his wife and children). The Angkar chief announced that the man and the woman, Phon and Heang, had been having an affair. (They had no proof but heard it and believed it to be so.) Angkar then asked Phon's wife to stand up and identify herself. Phon's wife was asked what should be done about it. His wife remained silent. The Angkar chief said that Phon and Heang were bad role models for the people and that they are the enemy against Angkar rule. Angkar does not allow for a man to have two wives. All marriages have to be approved by Angkar. (Before Khmer Rouge rule, it was not uncommon nor unacceptable for men to have more than one wife in the home.) Angkar reiterated that men are not allowed to have more than one wife and that these expectations were spoken of at many Angkar meetings prior to this.

I looked at the man and the woman in the center of the circle. They were both wet and muddy from planting in the fields, like I had been. Angkar asked those gathered for any comments. Nobody said anything. We knew that it was dangerous to speak up. Angkar decided to kill them both to use them as examples. Angkar asked us, *"Do you want to see how we kill them?"* They pulled Phon and Heang back outside of the circle, toward the back of Preh Vihear. The crowd was dispersed, and I headed back to the Preh Vihear. The killing was in progress. Angkar killed the man first. I watched as they knelt him down on the ground. He called out to his mother three times, crying, *"Mai, Mai, Mai,"* honoring his mother. A soldier took a bamboo stick and struck him hard on his neck a number of times. Phon's body flailed, then he lay flat. Two soldiers held him down while a third soldier cut open his abdomen and removed his gallbladder. The same torture was done to Heang. She remained silent. Angkar also removed her gallbladder. Because I was standing nearby (on my way to the Preh Vihear), one of the soldiers approached me and directed me to fetch a bowl of water from the pond. I got the bowl of water and was directed to pour the water over Angkar's bloody arms so they could wash. The soldiers had a split bamboo stick (used for hauling things) where they placed the two gallbladders inside to carry. I was asked by Angkar if I wanted one of the gallbladders. I replied that I did not. (There was a practice where gallbladders would be dried and used for medicinal purposes.)

Angkar left the two bodies where they were killed, amongst all of the blood and gore. They did not cover them. It was horrific. The dead bodies were located just off the steps of the Pre Vihear where the girls and I slept. A few of the girls and I went to the Chief of the Sub-Korng Chalatt and requested that the dead bodies be removed. The stench and their slaughtered corpses were painful to witness. The Sub-Korng Chalatt chief then asked the chief of the Sahakor (the elder camp that we were working at) to remove the bodies. Later that night, workers dug one grave in that very location and buried both bodies together, just off the steps of the Preh Vihear at Kean Kess Temple.

Those were the first murders I'd actually witnessed, but it wasn't the first time I'd seen people who were murdered by the Khmer Rouge. There were many murder victims of the Khmer Rouge whose bodies I'd seen discarded along the roadside on my exodus from Battambang. We'd all witnessed that: the elders, men, women, and children. I saw dead bodies in many places: floating in the canal, laying in the fields, and elsewhere. But this time, I witnessed the horror of the torture and killing. It haunted me. I was unable to sleep. I felt drained and deep emptiness of mind and spirit. None of us were permitted to voice how we were affected. We had to hold everything in. We at no time had the ability to denounce what Angkar said and did to anyone if we wished to survive. I had to push down my feelings at all times. All of us did.

Years later, when I first arrived in the United States, I enjoyed watching violent programs on television because oftentimes the good people triumphed over the bad people in the end. That's what I longed to see happen. My sponsor Glenda caught on to that and said that it wasn't a healthy thing to do. So began the long journey of my healing process.

The Killing Fields

While laboring in the fields, I could see the boys plowing the fields from a distance. The boys were given no plows or implements to do their job. Instead, they used their feet. The boys jumped up and down over and over in the muddy field to prepare the ground for planting. Once the fields were determined to be ready, the girls planted rice. As I watched these boys and young men jumping up and down to plow the land, I knew that life led by Angkar wasn't about equity at all, like the Khmer Rouge claimed. No, it was about torture. Where had all the plows gone? Where were the tractors? The cows? Why weren't they providing those things? But we were to remain mute. Nobody was allowed to ask these questions. Nobody was allowed to complain. Everybody had to remain silent and work. I witnessed one young man who was so emaciated and physically exhausted from jumping up and down to plow the field that he collapsed and died. Angkar forced all to work excessively hard. I believe that Angkar did this to weed out those who, prior to the Khmer Rouge, had been wealthy and had no farming experience. These people would not have the physical stamina or the farming experience to survive.

I worked with a girl named March on my team. We often worked side by side in the rice field. When we were digging the canal, March was never able to finish her work. She'd confided in me secretly that she was from the city and had never had to do any physical work. Her family had a housekeeper and a cook. March had been a student. Angkar kept their eye on her every day. They knew that her work was never completed. Of course, March had no farming experience at all. When those of us with experience planted the rice, we used a technique to keep the rice plant in place. We'd put the rice paddy root into the ground, then turn the root under, then pat the earth around it. March didn't know the proper technique. She was given no instructions. The day after she'd planted rice paddies, hers would be floating. Angkar knew that the floating rice paddies were hers.

Who Will Be Killed? Who Will Be Spared?

One day while March and I were working in the field together in the Kaung Village, two Khmer Rouge soldiers approached us and directed us to leave our work and join them for a meeting. The two soldiers, March, and I walked about half a kilometer through the field before reaching the road. A car was waiting for us. We were told to get into the car. The soldiers accompanied us to Roung Ampil Village where our meeting was to take place.

When we arrived, March was directed into one room and I into another. We were both interrogated. I was asked whether I'd known March previously. I did not and told them that. Next, they asked for my history. I told them that I grew up on a farm. Then I lied. I said I'd been farming all my life and that I'd never attended school. *"How do you feel about Angkar?"* they asked. Again, I lied. I said that I really liked Angkar, that I'd been very poor and had worked very hard but never got enough to eat. People looked down on my dad because he always wore black on the farm and now everybody wears black. I liked that. I told them I was happy. Angkar was helping to make my life better. I was still doing the same work that I'd always done. When my interview was done, the soldiers told me to come with them, that they wanted to show me the enemy.

I went with them and there was March. She stood there in front of me with her hands pulled behind her back and in hand-cuffs. Angkar spoke to me in front of March, saying, *"We have to get rid of her because she is not honest. She is not helpful, and she never finishes her work. She is against Angkar."* They repeated, *"March is the enemy."* Angkar said, *"We do not gain anything by keeping this person. If we take this person out of the Korng Chalatt we don't lose anything."*

This was in keeping with the official slogan of the Khmer Rouge: ***"To destroy you is no loss, to preserve you is no gain..."***

While I stood facing March, the soldiers took a plastic bag, placed it over her head, and tied it tightly around her neck. March was gasping and writhing for air. She was desperately trying to breathe, but she could not. I watched her die. Then her bladder let go. A soldier, who must have been fourteen or fifteen years old, laid her on the floor and then, with a knife, cut open her belly and pulled out her gallbladder. It was so bloody and unimaginable.

I was forced to witness the Khmer Rouge brutally murder my friend March. Then I fainted. I felt broken. I'd lost whatever spirit I'd been able to hang on to up to this point. I was in shock and completely overwhelmed. I was so fearful that Angkar would discover my lies and that I'd be their next victim. I felt that I'd never recover from witnessing their brutality. I knew that I'd never again be the person I once was. Afterward, Koeurn, a female soldier, gave me a ride on her bicycle back to the field. She spoke animatedly the entire time. She laughed. It seemed to me that Koeurn enjoyed watching them kill March. She instructed me that if anybody inquired about March, I was to tell them that she was moved to a different group. I was silent. I did not speak a word. And then I was back working in the rice field, that same afternoon, just hours after they killed March.

Personal Reflection

Since studying and practicing Buddhism for many years, when I reflect back to my friend March's murder and to the torture that I endured under the Khmer Rouge rule, I submit to my Buddhist teachings that wrongdoing committed in this, or a previous life results in consequences. Believing in karma helps me to find acceptance. I need not focus on the torture that I experienced. I believe that I must do good in my life. I pray for my friend March and feel tremendous compassion for her. She has atoned and has paid for the consequences for any past transgressions. I believe that March will receive a better life in a future life. In my self-healing, I reassure myself that I am now safe. I am at peace. My Buddhist practice journey helps me to not dwell on the deep sadness from my past. After immigrating to the US, my dad and I did not see one another for fifteen years, until I brought him to the US and we spoke together about karma. He too believed that in viewing the past in this way, the desire for revenge is released from our hearts.

Before my Buddhism practice, when I experienced the persecution and hardships during the Khmer Rouge rule, I would get extremely angry and upset. If given a chance at revenge, I would have desired to act in retaliation. But now, I no longer feel that way. Revenge is not good. Whatever wrongdoing the Khmer Rouge did to me will in turn befall them with consequences. That is karma. But if we retaliate, the bad karma will continue on and on.

1976

In 1976, I was reassigned to the cooking group. There were ten of us girls who did the cooking and food preparation for the 100 people living and working in camp. We made rice. First, we had to grind it to prepare it for cooking. Then we cooked it for our meals. It was our responsibility to forage the farm and the nearby village for edibles, including watergrass, water lilies, and vegetables. Sometimes Angkar provided the kitchen with salt and sometimes with prahok (a marinated fish fermented in salt and stored in a jar for a year). We collected firewood for cooking.

We were expected to have meals prepared and served in a timely fashion, according to the given schedule. There was no breakfast. Only lunch and supper were provided. As a food worker, we served lunch to the workers in the field. Our Korng Chalatt ate our evening meal at camp part of the time. Other times, when we were working past sunset in the field at night, we would deliver the evening meal to be eaten there.

Spies (Chlops) for the Khmer Rouge—Always in Search of "The Enemy"

While working, whether in the field or in food preparation, we were not allowed to have any personal conversations, to speak badly about Angkar, or to complain about our work or our living conditions. Everybody had to keep their family history to themselves and never share it. We knew we were at significant risk by sharing any details of our past. We were all aware that coworkers would disappear. We knew that they were being killed. Sometimes Angkar would tell us so. Angkar was searching for enemies every day. They would tell us, *"Our enemy has no weapon, but the enemy of Angkar does not work hard, and shows no responsibility for their job."* Someone may "steal" something (like a vegetable in the field or fruit from a tree because they were starving) and Angkar would tell us, *"They're the enemy."*

We ate together in silence. We constantly feared that spies (chlops) surrounded us, and conversation would bring us trouble. On the field, there were times when we could sneak in bits of conversation if we felt we weren't being watched. Personally, I did not share details of my life and history with anyone during this time. It would have been dangerous and life-threatening to share that I could read and write and that I had nearly completed my formal education. So even though I might be tired, I would smile, speak well of Angkar, and finish all the work assigned to me. I worked hard to prove to Angkar that I was truly a farm girl. And still at night, when we settled down to sleep surrounded by one another, we did not speak. We may have been weary, hungry, and lonely, but we did not cry.

1977—Kim Yean, My Sister, Dies from Starvation

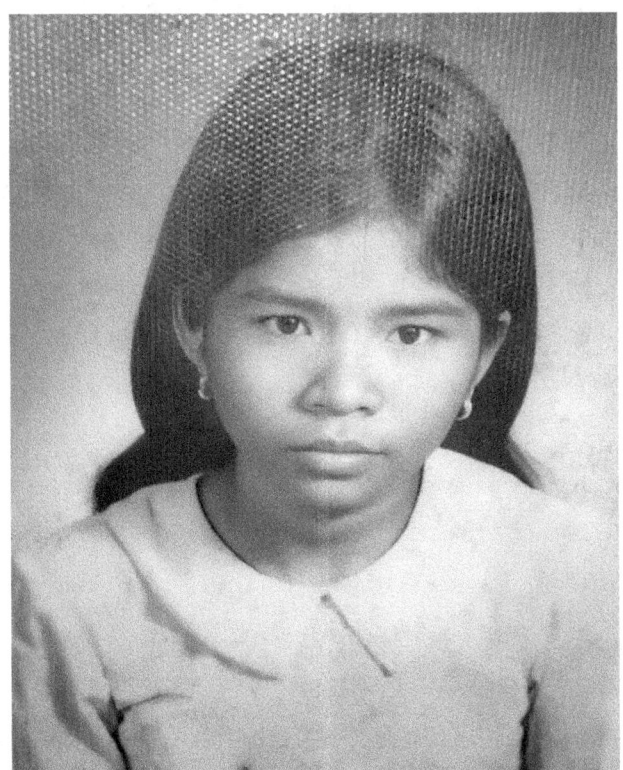

Kim Yean, Veera's sister, who died of starvation during the Cambodian Genocide. *Photo credit: Veera Som.*

One day I was selected to pick watergrass that grew wild in the rice field. While carrying my basket and picking the watergrass, I came across a girl I'd known from my home village. There was nobody else around, so we spoke with one another. She told me that prior to working here, she had been in the same Korng Chalatt as my sisters Channy, Navy, and Kim Yean. Then, she gave me heartbreaking news that my sister Kim Yean had passed away about three days before. She said Kim Yean had had diarrhea for many days and then died of starvation. With the news of losing my sister Kim Yean, I felt completely hopeless. I did not want to go on living. I was devastated. Now that I had learned where my other two sisters were, I desperately wanted to see them. I returned to the kitchen and told my leader that I'd just heard that my sister had died. I asked the Angkar lady in charge, with whom I'd developed a friendly relationship as I did an excellent job for her, for permission to visit my sisters. I missed them so much. Her response was: *"If you can make your sister come alive again, I'll let you go."*

Withdrawal to My Hammock. Refusal to Eat. Taken to Hospital with Severe Diarrhea

I was distraught. I walked back to the shelter and slept in my hammock. I just lingered there. I didn't eat. Angkar demanded that I return to work, but I refused. I no longer cared about anything. They could kill me if they wanted to. I didn't care. Two days passed by, and then I became extremely sick with diarrhea. I was given herbal medicine that looked like rabbit poop to help stop the diarrhea. We were located near the village of Kaung. Because I was so sick, the medical team members carried me, hammock and all, to a car, then drove me to the makeshift Borvel District Hospital, formerly a college. I was dropped off that first night in a room filled with very sick people. Angkar left me unattended and expected me to just sleep. There was no check-in of any kind. Nobody took my name or tended to me. The other patients and I slept together on mats on the floor. That night two people, a female and a male next to me, died and their bodies were taken away. While I lay there taking this all in, I started thinking, *"Since they did not register me, they have no record of my being here. Perhaps if I left, they wouldn't even notice? If they discovered that I was gone, maybe they'd think that I died like the others?"*

Escape from Hospital. Arrival at Herbal Medicine-making Camp

Early the next morning, I made my escape from the hospital. I had had nothing to eat or drink in days, but my desire to get away was strong. I knew that I was fairly close to the location where Kim Yean had been living. I learned that my sister Navy lived in Talten Village and that my sister Channy was in Mountain Kamping Pouy. I was told that my dad was now in Ta Kdol Village. Despite knowing where to find all of them, I was just too weak to travel to those locations. But I did walk as far as the village of Borvel. From a distance, I was able to see a small building that had a lot of wood piled up. This was a camp where herbal medicine was made. I saw people there chopping, chopping, and chopping wood. An idea came to me. I came up with a story that I had traveled to this place in search of medication for my asthma. An elderly man appeared to be running the operation.

He was a Krou Khmer, a traditional healer. He knew which herbal remedies to prescribe to treat various maladies. I approached him and told him that my team leader had given me permission to come there to drink the medicine until my health improved. He allowed me to remain to treat my asthma. Initially, upon arriving at this camp, I was very emaciated and weak. The elder took pity on me and initially gave me three days of rest and medicine to regain my strength. I boiled water, added the herb, and drank it three times each day. After this period, if I were to stay, Angkar required me to work. One of my jobs was to carry water to the camp from a nearby river. The elder gave me an easy job too, where I could sit while I worked. I chopped many vines and herbs. These were used to make IV fluids. First, they were steamed, then used as an intravenous drip for sick patients. There were a lot of people there working. Others, sick like me, were also given jobs while they stayed and took medicine.

I remained there for a month. The Khmer Rouge soldiers came to the camp every day to see who among us was feeling better and should return to their work camps. Of course, I had sent myself there. My work camp did not. I stayed clear of the Khmer Rouge but worried that I'd be discovered as being there illegally. I knew I couldn't stay indefinitely. It had been a comfortable place to be and to regain my strength. It was difficult to leave. After a month's stay, I asked the elder for his permission to return to my Korng Chalatt. He didn't want me to go, but I knew that it was time. I packed food for myself and left. I was not headed back to my Korng Chalatt like I'd said but was traveling on foot to where my dad lived in Ta Kdol Village.

Visit Dad, Stepmom, and Brother at Sahakor

At that time Heang Rithea, my youngest brother, who was then seven years old, was still living with my dad. When the Khmer Rouge came and evacuated everybody from their homes, my dad was a widower. Soon after, he married a woman who was also living in his camp. There was no ceremony. They lived in a Sahakor, an elderly camp, whose members did light work like caring for children and weaving baskets. A team in the Sahakor was assigned to cook for the community. A bell was rung at mealtimes and meals were eaten together in community. Couples were allowed to stay together as husband and wife. No one was allowed any personal possessions, nor did they have any personal food or cooking privileges in their own homes.

My father was fortunate that the people overseeing the Sahakor were not strict like they were in my Korng Chalatt. Parents living in nearby Korng Chalatts were allowed to send their children to the Sahakor for visits with their grandparents.

I arrived in Ta Kdol Village. A local villager directed me to my dad's cottage. When I arrived, I could see my brother Rithea just inside the door. He was whittling a stick with a knife. I was so happy to see my brother. It was about noon, and neither my father nor my stepmother were home. I called my brother's name: *"Rithea!"* He dropped his knife, and the bamboo stick he was carving. He was frightened and didn't speak with me. He'd heard that I had died and thought I was a ghost. Rithea ran to the community kitchen where my dad and stepmom were eating and reported to them that I had appeared to him at the house. A few hours later, my dad, stepmom, and Rithea returned home and studied me closely. They were in disbelief. They thought I was dead. They touched me, patted my hair, and counted my fingers. My stepmother exclaimed, *"A ghost does not have ten fingers! This really is Kim Soert!"* We were finally reunited and were overjoyed.

Soon after, my parents received permission from the Sahakor chief for me to stay with them and visit for three days. I was given a food ticket and allowed to join them for meals at the community kitchen. My dad cautioned me against sharing information at night, telling me, *"The walls have ears."* Spies were ever-present.

I was happy to be reunited with my family, but in turmoil over having to leave in just a few days. My dad wanted to hear about my experiences in the work camp. After we talked, he told the chief about my struggles with asthma and requested permission for me to remain at the sahakor to work, but the chief said no. He was concerned that my presence there might bring trouble to the sahakor.

My Sister Saly's One Night Visit with Dad

The following day I received a great gift. My sister Saly came to visit our dad while I was there. She hadn't known that I'd be there, so we were both surprised and elated to be together. She had permission to visit my dad for only one night before she had to return to her District Korng Chalatt. Saly told me that at her District Korng Chalatt that everyone was expected to work very hard both day and night but that the workers were given enough food to eat. Saly encouraged me to return to her camp with her. Dad agreed that this was a good idea and was hopeful that we'd be able to live together in the same camp.

Returned with Saly to Her District Korng Chalatt in Prasat

Village. My Sister Sarem Also Worked at This Camp

It was 1977. I left my dad's home and walked with Saly through the village and to the road. A car belonging to Angkar approached us. Saly was in good standing with the Angkar leadership from her camp. They gave us a ride back to her District Korng Chalatt. Saly told them that I had formerly lived in the Korng Chalatt Subdistrict but that I wished to relocate and work here in the District Korng Chalatt, to be close to my sister. I was allowed to stay and was assigned the same work as I did previously, digging the canal and farming the rice. We were now living and working at the same camp; but we rarely saw one another. My sister Sarem also worked at this camp, as a nurse, and distributed medication to sick workers. Saly cautioned me earlier that if I were to see Sarem, I was not to acknowledge her, nor tell anyone that she was my sister.

I worked day and night at the District Korng Chalatt and found that I was fiercely afraid of caterpillars. At night, we pulled rice paddies up from the field, gathered enough plants to make a bundle, and then replanted each bundle. A large electric light lit up the field and attracted many insects. As we worked, there were swarms of caterpillars all over the rice plants. A female soldier beat a woman worker with the butt of her gun because she jumped up and down screaming out of fear of the caterpillars. I too was deathly afraid of caterpillars but knew that I had to refrain from reacting to avoid reprisal. But there were so many caterpillars! They would crawl all over us as we worked the field. After a few days of extreme aversion to working in these conditions, I got used to them. I had no choice: either overcome my fear of touching and being touched by caterpillars or be beaten or killed. We worked until midnight and then walked back to the shelter. All of us young women were so exhausted when we arrived back at the shelter that we'd collapse, then fall asleep wearing our wet clothes. As a result, our inner thighs were often red, swollen, and infected. It was difficult working each day with such raw and infected upper thighs.

Big containers previously used for gasoline storage were cut in half and repurposed as toilets. Two boards were laid over the top, and plastic was wrapped around this makeshift toilet for privacy. The Khmer Rouge scattered a number of these toilets between rows in the rice fields so workers could use the toilet quickly and not waste precious work time. The Khmer Rouge purposefully assigned educated people, whom they hadn't yet killed, the dirty jobs of the fertilizer crew. These workers were given no soap for cleaning up. When toilets became full, two men carried them to a designated area where they dumped the slop and spread it out to dry in the sun. Once dry, the crew collected a specific kind of leaf to mix in with the slop to make fertilizer. The dried fertilizer was spread in the fields.

During the day shift, the kitchen workers delivered our lunch of rice to the fields at noon. We had 10 to 15 minutes to eat. We were given a bowl and a spoon but no cup. We got nothing to drink. For a drink of water, we sought out the clearest water in the field not being used for planting and scooped it into our hands and drank. The same was true when we became thirsty while working in the hot sun. There was a big jar of water located adjacent to the shelter. We could use our bowl to drink from the water jar there. Our bodies became immune to the poor water quality.

A member of my team suffered night blindness. She tried to explain her condition to Angkar to request being excused from night work as she couldn't see. Angkar didn't understand, and thought she was just lazy and pretending night blindness. So one night they tested her. They created a curvy maze and lined it with thorny branches. Angkar tested her to see whether she could successfully walk and remain on the curvy path. If she could do so, they believed it would prove that she did have night vision. But if she veered off the path and onto the thorny perimeter, they would believe her. This woman was bloodied from repeatedly veering off the path and stepping onto the thorny branches. Angkar finally believed her. She was removed from nighttime field work and assigned work in a well-lit area.

My sister Sarem and I saw each other regularly when she was delivering medication to workers in the field, but we did not speak or acknowledge one another. But, just seeing her lifted my spirits and made me happy. Sarem followed the rules and would never sneak into the shelter to see me, bring me food, or take any unnecessary risks, but my sister Saly did. Only supervisors were given shoes to wear. The shoes were made from car tires. As a field worker, I always worked barefoot. When it was hot, day in and day out, the ground became extremely dry and cracked, and so did my feet. Saly knew this and felt bad for me. She knew it was painful to work barefoot in these hot, dry conditions. One day she sprinted to me while I was working in the field to give me her shoes. Saly would rather be barefoot than see me, her older sister, suffer.

We lived in a community called Prasat Village. We slept from midnight to 5:00 a.m., then went back to work in the fields. Eventually, I got quite sick. I suffered with impetigo on the top of my head. This is a contagious bacterial skin infection that formed pustules and yellow crusty sores on my scalp. I also had head lice, a miserable condition that was extremely itchy and very contagious. Most of us were stricken with it at one time or another. We had no shampoo and were given no treatment for the head lice, so it lasted a long time. Thankfully, it eventually cleared up on its own, but while I had it, I was miserable.

Cleaning Rice Triggers a Severe Asthma Attack — Hospitalization

During the dry season/harvest season, one of the field workers' jobs was to spread the rice out on the ground, then a tractor drove over the rice to separate it from its shell. This job was done at night. During the day we harvested rice. Another task we performed at night was stirring up the straw to separate it from the rice. One hundred people in unison stirred up the straw. It was such a dusty operation. I wore a krama (scarf) to cover my nose and mouth, but despite that, I suffered a severe asthma attack while working. I was wheezing terribly and had to walk away. My sister Sarem led me back to the shelter and reported to Angkar that because of the very dusty conditions I was having an asthma attack. Despite my pronounced wheezing, Angkar didn't believe it. There was no medicine to treat my wheezing so it continued day and night. My breathing grew extremely labored. I was very ill. Eventually, Angkar took me to the make-shift hospital operating in the former Thma Koul College, located about six kilometers from Prasat Village. The hospital had no medicine that successfully treated my asthma. Given that, an experimental burning method was tried. Cotton balls were wound up very tightly and placed on my chest. Incense was then used to burn through cotton balls placed on my chest and other spots along my diaphragm. As this was done, I was told to take deep breaths. This was not done as torture, but as a healing method, but it didn't provide relief but rather worsened my condition. It was extremely painful, and I suffered second-degree burns, that became infected. It did nothing to improve my asthma. However, being away from the dusty culling process of the rice while recovering at the hospital for a few months gave my lungs time to recover.

During my convalescence at the hospital, a male patient also suffering from labored breathing, was located close by me. In hindsight, I think he likely had tuberculosis. One day I noticed that he carried a knife with him. The next day I learned that he'd passed away and saw that his knife was bloodied. He had slit his own throat and left a suicide note: *"I've decided to end my life. Nobody hurt me. I can no longer endure this prolonged suffering. Living is painful, and there's no medication to cure me. This is why I've decided to end my life."* He was about thirty years old, emaciated, and looked like a ghost.

Reflecting Back

"When I look back and share my story, I wonder why it is that I survived? Currently, I take medication every day to control my asthma. I don't understand how I survived. During this asthma episode in the makeshift hospital, I couldn't breathe for seven days. I received no supplemental oxygen and yet I survived. Each and every day while I worked on the farm and nobody was in close proximity to observe me, I would look to the sun in the sky and silently pray: Why do Cambodians kill our people every day and yet nobody comes to help us? Why don't Americans come to help? Why is it that others from around the world do not come to help? Don't they know that Cambodians are living like this every single day? While living at the District Korng Chalatt I felt a bit better about my situation because I saw my sisters often. That made a difference to me. But we were unable to talk to one another, nor tell each other that we loved one another, but we were not all alone.

My Brother Rithy Appears in Rice Field

One day while working in the rice field I looked up and there stood my little brother Rithy. I had not seen Rithy since the Khmer Rouge takeover more than two years before. Because nobody else was within earshot, Rithy said, *"Sister. I live over there."* My heart skipped a beat, and I whispered back to him, *"Oh my brother, what are you doing here?"* Rithy was living nearby in the Young Kids Team of eight-to ten-year-old children. The kids had many jobs, including taking care of the cow, cutting the grass, and, at this time, Rithy and his team's job was to create little dams along the walkways in between the rice fields to prevent water from escaping from one area to another. I stood up in the field and walked to a bathroom located on one of the walkways where he was working, and we had a chance to briefly visit there.

Rithy now knew where I was working, but we had to be careful not to acknowledge one another in the company of others for fear of reprisals. One day Rithy walked up to see me and tossed a mud pie at me and then just held his gaze with mine but didn't utter a single word. I didn't understand his actions but felt he was communicating something with me. When nobody was nearby, I examined the mud pie. Hidden inside the crusty mud pie, my little brother had carefully wrapped a leaf around a fish that he had cooked for me. His kind gift of freshly cooked fish filled my heart with gladness. I was thankful. Because nobody was nearby, I ate the fish right away. It was delicious. I hadn't eaten any cooked fish for a few years, since before the takeover by the Khmer Rouge. I'd only received rice to eat. Rithy knew that. I was moved by my little brother's generosity and ingenuity.

The Khmer Rouge weren't as strict with the children as they were with the young adults. The kids were allowed to pick and eat fruit from the trees or catch fish or crabs to eat without getting into trouble. They were allowed to build a fire on a nearby hill or alongside a tree adjacent to the rice fields and cook their fish, something we were never allowed to do. There were more gifts of cooked fish from Rithy to come, before his team eventually moved on.

Within my District Korng Chalatt, while working in the rice fields, we would see small crabs or small shrimp, but only when there were no Khmer Rouge or fellow workers around (because we couldn't trust anybody) could we wash this small morsel and eat it raw without being seen. If someone were to catch us, it could mean dire consequences.

My Friend's Cousin Mouy, Now Known as Dar, Turned Into Angkar as "The Enemy"

I recall the day in 1975 when the Khmer Rouge soldiers evacuated the city of Battambang, where I was living, how my roommate and I walked north with the crowd of people for 30 km until, at sunset, we stopped for the night in Thmey Village, where my dad's home was. The soldiers permitted the people to knock on doors to find shelter for the night or to sleep alongside the road. That night, in addition to my roommate and I finding shelter at my dad's home with my family, we welcomed a friend of mine, Vanney, whom I'd met in Battambang, her grandmother, and her cousin Mouy from Phnom Penn to stay the night. Mouy's dad had served as a commander in Cambodia's previous government's army, the Khmer Republic.

Fast forward to the present, 1977. Here I was at the District Korng Chalatt, working in the rice field, when I spotted my friend Vanney's cousin, Mouy. Mouy had since changed his name to Dar in an attempt to conceal his background, a frequent practice at that time. Dar was working on the men's team in the same location as that of my District Korng Chalatt. This was the first time I'd seen him since the day of the takeover in 1975. I learned that Dar was very skilled at fixing machines, including irrigators, motorcycles, tractors, and cars. He had developed a close relationship with the Angkar chief at his camp. Angkar was very fond of him. They were unaware of his family ties to the

Khmer Republic. Dar was welcome to come and go from the Angkar chief's home. He was given the privileges of a trusted friend.

Soon after I became aware of his presence in the camp, one of the men on his work team, who had been a former classmate of Dar's from Phnom Penn, became jealous of Dar's special privileges and of the friendly relationship that Dar had with the Angkar chief. This former classmate reported to the Angkar chief that Dar was the enemy. He exposed Dar's history and background to Angkar, and soon the chief began asking Dar questions. Dar refused to reveal the truth, but he knew then that somebody had betrayed him. He knew that his life was in jeopardy, and he acted quickly.

Before Dar's identity as *"the enemy"* was made known to his Angkar friends, he paid a visit to one of their homes. While visiting with his Angkar friend's wife, and with her husband not there, Dar grabbed a gun that was hanging on the wall, and the ammunition beside the gun, and took it against his friend's wife's protests. The woman pleaded with him not to take it, saying that her husband would kill her for allowing him to take it. She had loved Dar like a brother. But Dar knew that he was in danger and left with the gun. He didn't hurt her. He fled with the gun on his motorcycle, and his friend, the gun owner, appeared and chased after him to retrieve his gun. Dar shot his friend in the shoulder, injuring but not killing him. From there, Dar returned to the rice field where I was working. Dar, with his gun drawn, demanded that all of us workers, both male and female, immediately stop working and do as he say. He was looking for revenge against whomever betrayed him and revealed his background to the Angkar chief. He demanded that all of us line up in one straight line. He looked very menacing and kept his gun pointed towards all of us.

I was frozen with fear that he'd direct his wrath at me because I knew of his past and thought that he might see me as a threat to him. I believed that Dar was about to shoot me. But then, Dar spotted his classmate from Phnom Penn. He aimed his gun at him and shouted, *"I know it was you who reported my background to Bong [brother] Som!"* Then he pulled the trigger and killed him.

Immediately afterward, Dar jumped back onto his motorcycle and drove to the village of Thma Koul. This is where Dar's cousin, my friend Vanney, and their grandmother were living. By this time, Dar knew that many Khmer Rouge soldiers there would know that he had turned against them. What they didn't know was whether he had a group of men with him or whether he was alone. Dar quickly made his way into the building, attacking any soldiers in his path attempting to stop him. Some he killed with a knife; others he shot with his gun while making his way up onto the roof. An army truck unloaded many soldiers onto the street to pursue him. The Khmer Rouge soldiers ordered him to get down from the roof, but he didn't comply. He was not going down without a fight. Soldiers attempted going up the stairs to catch him and Dar killed as many of the soldiers as he could, a total of ten people in all.

Once the Khmer Rouge captured Dar, they bound his hands together, tied him to a car, and dragged him behind the vehicle until he was dead. Then the soldiers captured Dar's grandmother and his cousin Vanney. They killed them both. Before killing

Vanney, the Khmer Rouge soldiers repeatedly raped her and afterwards bragged about it.

Once Dar and his family were killed, the Khmer Rouge conducted an exhaustive search of all workers who had known Dar and who may have had a relationship with him. The Khmer Rouge began killing these workers one by one. We would be out working in the field, and a black Isuzu vehicle would drive up alongside us on the road. Soldiers would step out of the vehicle carrying a list of people they wanted to question about Dar that day. A soldier would call the names on the list. Those called would step up to the car, their hands were bound before entering the vehicle, and they were taken away for questioning. In most cases, these people were not returned to the field and were presumed to be dead.

The Khmer Rouge held daily meetings to report to us workers how many people they had captured and killed because they happened to know Dar. One day when I had finished my work for the day and was walking toward Prasat Village carrying the basket I used in the field, the Isuzu vehicle pulled up beside me on the road. This time, they called my name. I was told to get into the car, but first my hands were bound and I was blindfolded. I entered the car and was taken to a building for questioning. Their questions were about how I knew Dar. At that time, I had just recently moved to the District Korng Chalatt, and I told them that. I said that I'd met Dar here at camp but that I didn't know him well. I told them that I had never been to Phnom Penn (which was true) and that I was a farm girl. I said I was happy with how I was currently living. I had said similar things when they interrogated me about my friend March. During this time, I felt certain that my interrogator would kill me, just like they killed all those who were questioned and killed before me. After all, I did know Dar, his cousin, and their grandmother. I didn't admit to that but didn't know if somebody else might know that and had reported me. I really believed that this was it. I would be killed, and I had made peace with that. Living was extremely hard. Every day I experienced high anxiety. I did not have enough food to eat. It was so hard on my body, mind, and spirit. I felt that I had suffered enough. Life has become devoid of meaning. I just didn't want to witness any more suffering. Angkar hurt people every day. I witnessed this. No hope remained. Except, I did hold onto one hope: that I wouldn't be tortured before I died. And I regretted that if I were killed and not returned to camp that my sister Saly would be devastated.

Since the interrogations about Dar began, Saly would frequently sneak into my sleeping shelter at night just to make sure that I was still safe. We could not talk. She would just touch my foot and whisper: *"Sister, are you okay?"* This was a risky thing that she did.

Following my interrogation, the soldiers left me alone overnight and I was left to wonder: *"When will they return to kill me?"* I managed to get through the night because I was exhausted; I'd been given nothing to eat. I cried myself to sleep. When morning came, I was told by a soldier: *"Come with me. I'll send you back."* I cannot describe how I felt, but I was thankful to be alive. I did not want to die.

When I returned to camp, I worried a great deal about Saly. Saly knew Dar very well. At every meeting Angkar said that they still had many people yet to investigate. But, in the end, Saly was not questioned. Upon completion of the interrogations as to who knew Dar, 280 people were said to be killed who were determined to either have known or had been friends with Dar.

1978—New Angkar Leadership in Camp

I was 23 years old in 1978 when new leadership arrived at our Korng Chalatt from southern Cambodia, replacing the former Angkar leadership. The reason this occurred was not explained. Conditions improved in camp. The new Angkar spoke less about doing investigations and looking for *"the enemy"* at our daily meetings. Witnessing people being handcuffed and murdered subsided. I felt a glimmer of hope return. Our eating rations improved and began to include portions of cooked rice, not just the rice soup, which provided us with little sustenance. Angkar became less strict and began allowing the sick to rest. These were noticeable and welcome improvements to our daily living conditions. We welcomed the changes.

About this time Angkar decided that women 21 years and older should marry and begin to have children. They began pairing couples up and arranging these marriages. One hundred couples were paired up by Angkar between the male and female Korng Chalatts. One ceremony was held to officiate these mass marriages. Prior to this ceremony I protested the marriage plan made for me with Angkar. I explained that I resisted the marriage plan because of my chronic asthma, claiming that my lungs were weak and that I wasn't well. Although Angkar countered that if I were to marry, I'd be able to stay in one location with my husband and would not have to work so hard traveling from one work site to another. However, Angkar did grant my request. I preferred to remain in the traveling Korng Chalatt rather than marry a stranger.

During the dry season (harvest time) I received a new assignment of milling the rice. About 30 of us workers operated the hand-milling machines day and night, preparing enough rice for the kitchen to cook daily. This was a four-step process. I worked with batches of rice.

First, I poured rice into the hand-milling machine and stirred and stirred each batch round and round to remove the outer skin, also known as the rice's first skin, known as the amkan in Cambodia. Once the amkam is removed, the rice then has the appearance of brown rice. Secondly, I pounded the brown rice to remove its brown skin. Then I separated the brown rice skin, known as the kontouk, which at this point is a powder, and collected the kontouk to be used later as feed for the pigs. Nothing was wasted. Lastly, I bundled the white rice, and it was returned to the kitchen for meal preparation.

Our Korng Chalatt produced an abundant amount of rice. However, Angkar provided the workers with small rations, depriving us of getting a sufficient amount to eat. Although, make no mistake, Angkar made sure that *they* always had more than enough to eat. In addition to rice, Angkar ate ducks, pigs, and chicken. Camp workers were never given meat to eat. But now that the new Angkar leadership was in place, we began receiving cooked fish and vegetables in addition to the rice. Salt was provided as well.

My Suitor Named Sung

My new job of milling rice was a better job for me than working in the rice fields. Now I work inside a building, not outside, which keeps me out of the rain and the hot sun. Each of us on my team had our own milling machine. Our workstations were separated by walls, a bit like cubicles, which gave us each some privacy. I both worked and slept in my workstation. Each day the cooks sent someone to each of our workstations to deliver rice for us to mill as well as to collect the rice already milled. Sung was the young man assigned to visit my workstation. He was from the men's team who were responsible for planting the sugar cane and raising the ducks. Sung and I had brief chats when he came to drop off and collect the rice. Soon he began bringing me gifts of food each day. Sometimes it was a boiled egg and other times, maybe a stick of sugar cane. The walls in my workstation kept others from looking on. A romance blossomed between us and eventually Sung fell in love with me. Then one day Sung told me that he was planning to ask Angkar to have someone on his behalf request my hand in marriage. I was glad that he shared this with me beforehand. I did like Sung but was not ready to get married. I said to him: *"Sung, if you love me then you'll wait for me."*

March 1979—Khmer Rouge Overthrown by Vietnamese Forces

And then it happened. The Vietnamese Liberation occurred in March 1979, toward the end of the dry season, about three months following the arrival of the new Khmer Rouge leadership at camp. On that first day, I was milling rice and looked up and saw Khmer Rouge soldiers running west away from the District

Korng Chalatt in the direction of the Cambodia–Thailand border. Then about noon, I saw the Vietnamese soldiers driving their tanks along Highway 5. I heard them shouting, *"Di Vay Nha! Di Vay Nha!"* (Go Home! Go Home!). Given Angkar's quick departure on foot, and the Vietnamese soldiers' arrival and proclamation announcing for us to go home, it appeared to me and the other workers that the Khmer Rouge had lost their reign in leadership of Cambodia. A huge sense of relief settled over the Korng Chalatt that our days of oppression and torture had finally come to an end. However, this announcement was not coming to us from our communist Cambodian leadership, but rather from the Vietnamese Army. I was skeptical. I'd studied Cambodian history in school. I knew that historically Cambodia did not trust Vietnam. Our countries had a long history of war between us. When I saw the Vietnamese descending on the Korng Chalatt, my natural reaction was one of fear that the Vietnamese would overthrow our government. But then I also felt hopeful that the Vietnamese soldiers wouldn't torture us the way that the Khmer Rouge were doing.

A group of about ten Khmer Rouge soldiers came to the milling area near where I was working and sat there discussing the situation and what was happening. I overheard snippets of their conversation: *"What should we do? Where should we go?"* After strategizing for a while, these Khmer Rouge soldiers left quickly, departing westward. There was excitement within the Korng Chalatt. A universal sigh of relief occurred with the Vietnamese soldiers' arrival and with the fleeing of many of the Khmer Rouge soldiers. Some workers enthusiastically let go of long pent-up emotions from captivity and shouted in jubilation! They let down their guard, the caution that all of us in camp had practiced for so long. Now, expressions of joy that the Khmer Rouge Army had been defeated were shared. Unfortunately, this turned out to be reckless behavior. The presence of Khmer Rouge soldiers still existed around camp. Khmer Rouge and Vietnamese soldiers were actively shooting at each other. For those that openly celebrated the Khmer Rouge demise, they were shot and killed before the Khmer Rouge soldiers ran away. These oppressed Cambodian people had worked long and hard under the Khmer Rouge tyranny. But, because these workers had embraced their liberation with jubilation before the last of the Khmer Rouge soldiers had fled our Korng Chalatt, they lost their lives.

Much chaos and confusion took place at camp. I was needed in the field and kept my mouth shut and continued working despite the fighting around me between the Khmer Rouge and the Vietnamese soldiers. The workers were not their targets. Before long that same day, the Khmer Rouge had completely evacuated camp, and the Vietnamese soldiers moved out.

Departing the Work Camp in Search for Our Father

The next day my sisters Saly and Sarem found me at my workstation. Together we packed up salt, fish, rice, cooking utensils, and clothing for our journey. We talked and considered our options before moving on. We hadn't been able to converse like this since the Khmer Rouge takeover in 1975. We asked ourselves, *'Should we go first to see our father at his Sahakor, or should we travel directly to our father's house in Thmey Village?'* My sisters and I decided to first find our father. We learned that he lived in Kabar

Krorbey Village. Our journey there would lead us westward in the same direction as that which the Khmer Rouge had fled. We figured that if we traveled in the same direction as the Khmer Rouge soldiers did, that if our paths crossed with theirs, they'd assume that we supported them. We began our journey. Seven of us departed together, including my friend Sung. I asked him, *"Why do you want to come with us? Don't you want to go and find your family?"* There was much I didn't know about Sung. We had never been allowed to converse freely. Sung told me that he had no family. His family had all been killed. Sung told me that he loved me and wanted to remain with me.

We did not walk on the highway. Both the Khmer Rouge and the Vietnamese soldiers were traveling on the highway, and it was a dangerous route to take. Instead, we hiked through farms and fields. The first night we slept under the stars beneath a tree. The following day we walked and walked until we reached my father's Sahakor. The Vietnamese had not yet arrived in this village.

My sisters and I were the first to inform our father that our camp had been liberated by Vietnamese soldiers and that our camp's Khmer Rouge soldiers had fled. Our group now consists of my two sisters and me, Sung, a friend of ours, and her suitor. We asked our father if the six of us could stay with him. My father requested permission from the chief of the Sahakor, and his permission was granted. News of the demise of the Khmer Rouge soldiers from our Korng Chalatt began to circulate in the Sahakor.

My Love for Sung

Sung introduced himself to my father. He knelt before him in sompeah (palms together showing respect) and told my father, *"I love your daughter. That's why I've come with her. When the war and unrest dissipate, I request permission to marry your daughter. In the meantime, I ask if I could stay at your home to remain close to Veera because I love her, and I have no family."* My father gave Sung his permission.

Soon after, when I had completed my work in the field, I returned home and sought confirmation from my father that Sung would be allowed to stay. Privately, my father told me that he was embarrassed that I had brought a man home with me and that he didn't approve of Sung and I staying in his house together. My father also said that he had not yet decided whether he would grant his permission for Sung to marry me. He wanted to get to know Sung better before he made that decision. Sung would need to find somewhere else to live. That evening, when Sung returned from harvesting rice, I told him what my father said. Sung was understanding. My father wished to adhere to traditional Cambodian culture. I was his oldest living daughter. His expectation was that a representative from my suitor's family would come to him to request permission for my suitor to marry his daughter. But the extraordinary conditions of wartime made this an impossibility for Sung.

Not only was there turmoil surrounding us with the Vietnamese invasion, but this situation with Sung was stressful. I love Sung. He could not stay with me and my family, but I didn't know where to send him. He was not from here, but rather from southeastern Cambodia along the Vietnam border. My father's sister, a widow, lived two kilometers away. My father agreed to let Sung and I pay her a visit. Sung and I, along with my sisters Saly and Sarem, walked to my Aunt Yeen's home to visit her. I shared our love story with her: how Sung and I had met; his desire to marry me in the camp; his family circumstances and his desire to accompany me home to meet my father; and, most importantly, our love for each other. I asked Aunt Yeen if Sung could stay with her. Aunt Yeen genuinely cared for me and wished to see me happy. She welcomed Sung to live with her in her home.

Very soon after, my sisters Channy and Navy and my little brother Rithea arrived at my father's house. Our family was reunited. All but my sister Kim Yean had survived the communist Khmer Rouge occupation. My father, knowing that the Vietnamese army had liberated my camp, also knew that it was just a matter of time before liberation would come to his Sahakor. He began preparations immediately for the day we would leave to return to our home. About two weeks later, we heard fighting nearby. It sounded like the shooting was coming from my Aunt Yeen's home. Because her home was so close to the road, I was very worried for my aunt and Sung's safety. The following day, the Communist Khmer Rouge evacuated my father's Sahakor. The time had arrived. My father, stepmother, siblings, and I were going home. We traveled on foot for two days to get there. Respecting my father's authority, I did not ask him to wait for Sung to join us. He would not have accepted any questioning from me.

Dad and Stepmom, Heng Touch, sister Navy, her children Pisith and Kanika, and Saly. *Photo credit: Veera Som.*

Together My Family Returned to Our Pre-war Home in Thmey Village

When we arrived at my father's home, we found it occupied. Others who had fled the camps had arrived before us. We tried telling them that it was our house, but they would not believe us. We stayed outside the house for a few days, and then our former neighbors arrived. They acted as witnesses for my father and confirmed that the property belonged to him. My father did the same for the neighbors. The occupants left, except for an elderly woman and her son who had nowhere else to go. My father allowed her son to build a small shelter next to our home where they could live.

Woman sifting rice from straw using basket. *Photo credit: Sokrey.*

A few days later, my step-mom was sifting rice outside in front of our home. Our home sat close to Highway 5. She spotted Sung walking along the road. My stepmother quickly put her basket down and ran into the house, crying, *"Veera, Sung is walking down the road!"* I was so excited and ran to catch up with him. He had come looking for me! We were overjoyed to be to-gether. We spoke awhile outside. Sung was apprehensive to see my father and uncertain whether he would be welcome. We agreed that my father wouldn't allow him to stay. Sung had a friend living about six kilometers north of us, and he said that he would stay there. Then we walked inside together, and my dad and Sung had a talk. I gave them privacy but could hear bits and pieces of their conversation. Sung said that he was originally from the village of Prey Veng, located in southeastern Cambodia near the Vietnam border. Sung told my father that while he was studying at university in Phnom Penn that American forces had dropped bombs on his home village. His parents and his family had taken shelter underground, yet tragically, his entire family were killed by the bombing. Sung shared that he accompanied me to northwestern Cambodia where I'm from because he loves me, and he no longer has family to return to in Prey Veng. When the two of them finished talking, I accompanied Sung outside to say goodbye. Neither Sung nor my father recalled their conversation with me at that time.

Sung moved in with his friend and returned often to visit me. My father was not happy to see him. I know it had less to do with anything Sung had said or done, but that my father knew nothing about his family. This was something Sung had no control over. He couldn't change those circumstances. Sung didn't have family that could represent him in asking for my hand in marriage, nor did he have any money to contribute to prepare for a wedding celebration. It was Cambodian tradition that the man and his family paid the wedding expenses.

Opened a Roadside Vegetable Stand Business

My family and I started a business selling vegetables and grocery store items at our own roadside vegetable stand. Sung began stopping by the grocery stand on his motorcycle to visit me there, rather than visiting me at my father's home. One day my dad rode his bicycle by the grocery stand and saw Sung leaning on his motorcycle and speaking with me while I was working. We weren't alone. Many people surrounded us. Sung greeted my father, offering him sompea.

When I returned home, my father was livid and forbade me from seeing or speaking with Sung again, saying, *"Sung is a man that comes from nowhere."* In my family's very traditional culture, when a suitor comes from a distant location and his parents and relatives are unknown, then their daughter is not allowed to marry him. This was my father's position. He had made up his mind. I cried and cried and had sleepless nights. I was in love with Sung, but I knew now that Sung would not be getting my father's permission to marry me.

My Asthma

My asthma worsened. My health issues kept me from selling at our grocery stand. I'd have asthma attacks that lasted all night long, and I suffered severe breathing difficulties. My sisters would go out and track down asthma medicine for me. The medicine would provide relief, but then I'd run out and my severe symptoms would return. Living close to the dusty road was problematic, and our cooking smoke was a significant irritant as well.

CHAPTER 3

RESETTLEMENT CAMPS AT THE CAMBODIA/THAILAND BORDER

1981—My Initial Journey to the Border

Goods were being smuggled back and forth at the Thailand border daily. It was from the smugglers that I'd get the medicine I needed to control my asthma. My family continued with our grocery stand business. Gold was exchanged for merchandise as there was no currency yet in circulation in our village. Many villagers began taking journeys to the Thai border with the intent to relocate abroad. Through the smugglers, we learned of foreign organizations, including ARC (American Refugee Committee), that provided food, medicine, and aid to Cambodian refugees. Because I was chronically sick with asthma, my cousin (a smuggler) and I decided to travel to the border to purchase asthma medicine. Both my family and I knew that traveling to the border was dangerous. Despite that, my father permitted me to go. I left home with the intention of returning. My cousin and I rode together on a bicycle and alternately walked. After two or three days of traveling, we made it to Rithysen Camp (a Khmer resettlement camp at the Thailand border) unharmed.

Hospitalized at the ARC (American Refugee Committee) Hospital for Asthma Treatment

Inside the camp, I came across a family that I knew from my village. They welcomed me to stay with them. Soon after arriving, I ended up as a patient in the ARC Hospital in camp because of my asthma. ARC treated me with daily asthma medication. Once my symptoms began to dissipate, I secretly began cutting back on my dosage of prescribed asthma meds and would save the rest.

Returned Home to Thmey Village

After three to four months, I'd collected about 100 asthma pills, and my cousin had replenished his supply of goods to bring back home to sell. This was the way he made a living. Fortunately, our journey back home was without incident.

By this time, the living conditions in our village had begun to improve. It became easier to find aminophylline, my asthma medicine.

Farewell to Sung

Sung continued living nearby and was doing security work in the village. I had never had an opportunity to tell him that my father had forbidden me to see him again, so I wrote him a letter. I told Sung that I loved him and that my first reaction to my father's decision against permitting me to marry him was to run away with him. But, after much back and forth, I knew that I wouldn't be able to do that. I'm the oldest of the unmarried sisters. I explained that my father is well-known in the village and has a good reputation in the community. Running away with a man my father does not approve of would diminish my father's stature in the community. There was nothing I could do. I could not have him come with me across the border either. I must be obedient to my father. I closed my letter telling him, *"Please don't wait for me, Sung. This is an impossible situation for us. Because you no longer have family; it won't work between us. -Veera. I do love you."*

I received a return letter from Sung. My sister Sarem delivered it to me, after she read it first. He said he understood my decision to respect my parents' wishes and that he still thought I was a good person. He was sad and felt hopeless over losing me as well as his family. *"Meeting you, Veera, gave me hope. Now my hope is gone.* I didn't know that my fiancé was like a firefly. *One day I will get good news from you. Other days I get bad news from you."* His letter expressed hurt and regret but also understanding. Sung concluded saying: *"I will move far away. You'll never see me again."* My heart was broken.

I learned that Sung moved to Battambang. About a year later I heard that he was now married and working as a policeman. Then later, when our family was preparing for Saly's wedding celebration, I traveled to Battambang to purchase wedding supplies. I wanted to see Sung. I located him in the city. We met and talked. He had moved on.

The conditions in my home village continued to improve. We now have currency. The markets had expanded their inventory and were carrying a greater selection of food and medications. Schools were starting up again, and progress was being made in returning to life as we knew it before the Khmer Rouge occupation. I started hearing that the Cambodian refugee camp in Thailand was enabling some Cambodian refugees with the opportunity to immigrate to a "third country" i.e., Canada, France, and the United States. (first country: Cambodia; second country: Thailand; and third country.) I was educated and had dreams of a career in the medical field. I was ready to pursue my dreams in hopes of a better future. Fighting continued between the warring factions—the Khmer Rouge, Thai soldiers, Khmer Resistance soldiers, and the Vietnamese soldiers. I dreamt of an escape from the brutality of war. I wanted to further my education. I wished to learn English. The possibility of immigrating to a third country inspired me.

1982—Decision to Return to Khmer Resettlement Camp

In 1982, I decided that I wanted to journey to the border once again. I knew that it could be a dangerous journey to undertake. Between my village and the Thai border, Khmer Rouge soldiers continued their fighting with the Vietnamese army. Many land mines were scattered along the route. I requested my father's permission to return to the Rithysen Resettlement Camp. I attempted to justify my request: 1) I would need asthma medication for the rest of my life and didn't want my family to carry the burden of that medical expense indefinitely; it pained me to take what little extra money my family earned from sales at our grocery cart to pay for my medication; 2) I was unable to work on the farm or at our family grocery cart because of my asthma condition; 3) I was ready to take responsibility for myself; I was a 27 year old adult. But my father forbids me to go. Despite his refusal to give me permission, I resolved to go anyway. I would run away, then travel with a guide to the Khmer Resettlement Camp. My cousin was no longer a smuggler, so I would have to hire a travel guide to escort me to the border. Because my father had forbidden me to go, asking him for the money I needed to pay my guide wasn't an option. I could not disclose my plans to my siblings because I was quite certain they would tell my dad. Because I had no money to pay for a guide, the only option that I could see was to take a gold earring that belonged to my family and use it as "payment" for my guide's services.

Farewell Letter to My Father and My Family

It was currently the dry season, October 1982. I made advance arrangements with a guide to meet me on a given day at a specified location away from my house to avoid being seen leaving my home. I packed up food and clothing for my journey and left a letter under my pillow for my father and family that read:

Dear Father and Sisters:

By the time you read my letter I'll be gone. You may think badly of me, Dad, as your daughter. I'm sorry that I left home without your permission. I know that you told me that I might not be safe at the camp. Because I have asthma, I will require medication indefinitely. I don't want to depend on my family to take care of my needs any longer. I took a gold earring that belongs to the family to pay a guide to escort me to the Khmer Resettlement Camp at the border. Please forgive me Dad, and my sisters. If I get the chance, I will come back to visit you." - Your daughter and Sister, Veera

Departed from Home with a Cambodian Travel Guide

I left home and walked about a kilometer, where I met up with my travel guide. We bicycled to Serey Sophorn. When we arrived, others were waiting to join us. After sleeping there overnight, my guide, me, and five others started out again. A young child and a nine-month-old baby were part of our travel group. I didn't know the others, as we were from different provinces. We walked all morning to cross the village and then proceeded into the forest. We knew that Vietnamese soldiers were guarding the Cambodian/Thailand border. "If we were to encounter them," our guide explained, "the Vietnamese soldiers would turn us back." We trusted our guide's experience in traveling this route. He knew certain areas where no guards were expected to be posted, and that's the route that we took. While walking in the forest, it was imperative that we walked in a single file, with each step that we took placed in the footsteps of our guide and of those who had walked before us so as to avoid stepping on landmines.

Our travel group walked for half a day and then stopped to eat the provisions that we'd packed and carried. Once we'd eaten, we continued walking. The nine-month-old baby was crying a lot. Our guide was concerned that the crying baby would draw the attention of the soldiers and robbers in the nearby area and jeopardize our safety. Our guide instructed the baby's mother to bunch up her krama (scarf) very tightly and to pack it inside the baby's mouth to stifle his crying. The weather was hot and humid; the journey was long; and the baby was tired, hungry, and uncomfortable. We walked into the night, using the moonlight to illuminate our path. When the canopy of trees kept the moonshine from lighting our trail, our guide used his flashlight. He was vigilant in watching for signs of a worn path, trampled leaves, or broken twigs so that we stayed on a safe path away from the landmines.

Encountered Danger on the Journey

With trepidation, our guide spotted robbers just up ahead. They were Khmer Resistance soldiers. They were pointing their guns outstretched in our direction. Our guide first approached them alone, telling them that this group he was leading was poor. He pledged that whatever money we had between us we would relinquish it to them. Then, with their guns pointing directly at us, they said, *"Give us the money and valuables you have with you, or we'll kill you."* My fellow travelers turned over their valuables. I had nothing to give. I had already given my gold earring to my guide.

War is ugly. I have already survived many years of it. I'd been separated from my loved ones. I had my freedom stripped away from me and worked day and night for the Khmer Rouge, who were ruthless and harsh. I witnessed innocent people murdered at the hands of Khmer Rouge soldiers. I'd endured starvation and brainwashing. I was hospitalized multiple times and witnessed daily violence at camp. Was there no end to it? This time, atrocity was committed against me. The perpetrators were the Khmer Resistance soldiers. Because I had no valuables to give them, they led me off the path and away from my guide and travel group.

They ordered me to undress. Because private body cavities were being used to hide gold or diamonds, they examined my body and then sexually assaulted me. It was evening and past dark. I survived. Had this occurred during daylight and I had been able to see their faces; they would have killed me because I would have been able to identify my attackers. I was physically and emotionally ravaged. I got up and got dressed. I joined my traveling group, and we continued on our journey.

While hiking through the forest, two or three times we heard explosions from land mines being set off. People like us were losing their lives as they attempted to seek a better future.

Registered at Rithysen Resettlement Camp

Our travel group reached Rithysen Resettlement Camp the following October day in 1982 at about noon. It had taken us one day and one night to get there. The camp was under the leadership of Soeung San. The chief of the quarter registered our group upon arrival. The baby was hurried off to the camp hospital. His lips were swollen and sore because of being muzzled for the many hours of our travels. We received a supply of food, and the supplies needed to build shelter. Since I was at camp alone, I declined the building supplies offered. I explained that my cousin Kim Sur was a resident at camp and that I would look for her in the hopes of staying there with her, her husband, and her child. There were hundreds and hundreds of simply constructed homes inside the camp. After about a week of searching, I found my cousin, Kim Sur, who was from my mother's side of the family. She and her husband agreed that I could stay with them.

My Cousin Kim Sur Welcomed Me to Their Family Home

Kim Sur worked as a nurse for the American Refugee Committee Hospital (ARC). The ARC Hospital arranged for their Cambodian staff's homes to be located close by the hospital. We lived just next door. Initially, I remained home each day to care for Kim Sur's baby while she was at the hospital working.

When Picking Up My Asthma Meds, I'd Linger at the ARC Hospital

I picked up my medicine at the hospital. Each time I was there for a pickup, I enjoyed getting acquainted with the American workers. I'd linger there to listen and learn the English language. It was the American Refugee Committee staff that provided the medical care at camp. The food and shelter were provided by the United Nations High Commissioner for Refugees (UNHCR).

Thai soldiers guarded the camp. After arriving, we were required to remain inside the camp borders at all times. Rithysen Resettlement Camp was located on the Cambodian side of the Thailand border. We were not permitted to come and go freely. Camp housing was built by the occupants from bamboo and thatch. Some might include sheets of plastic or tarps in their construction. Our homes were small. The American workers didn't sleep at camp. The ARC staff arrived in the morning and left for town each day at 5:00 p.m.

1983

I enjoyed living so close to the ARC Hospital. I started spending as much time as I could there. I was permitted to walk freely throughout the hospital and observe the care being provided. Soon I began making friends with the American staff. I was eager to learn English. I learned that ARC trained Cambodian camp residents in various positions. Because American staff weren't at the hospital in the evenings and overnight, once trained, the Cambodian staff members covered those shifts.

I Was Invited and Began Classes to Become a Medical Staff Volunteer

The ARC Hospital had both American staff and Cambodian staff in leadership positions. Mary Beth Brown, an American staff volunteer, asked whether I'd be interested in becoming a hospital worker. I was definitely interested. I first needed to get permission from the Cambodian supervisor at the hospital. The Cambodian supervisor required that, prior to beginning medical training, I needed to earn a certificate from the Politics School, under the leadership of Chea Thach. This was a six-month course of study on the culture of the camp, including soldier training and general knowledge about war and morality.

Each person in camp was allotted only 25 liters of water per day. The lack of adequate available water led to poor hygiene in the camp. Many people in camp suffered from skin conditions, including scabies, impetigo, and abscesses. One of my first assignments at the hospital was to clean babies with scabies. The water truck from Thailand arrived in camp each day and pumped water into the big water tank. The water supply was then distributed to each quarter group leader, who then distributed the daily allotment of water to each household, who would then budget their daily water between the uses of drinking, cooking, bathing, and cleaning. It was not enough.

Food rations for the women and girls in camp were managed by food cards that were distributed every three months. Women were given rice and other food items by simply showing their food card. Men were not given food cards. Neither men nor boys were provided with food provisions in camp. Men were forced to either sneak out of camp to buy food for themselves and their sons or purchase food from vendors that sold food and other items in camp. The Thai baht was the currency used. People in camp somehow found ways to have money. Relatives of persons in camp who were already living in third countries would forward money by mail to American workers at their living quarters outside of camp, who would then deliver it to those persons in camp.

Classes taught at the ARC Hospital included three levels of medical training: (1) Health Worker, (2) Nursing, and (3) Medic. Because I'd been volunteering at the hospital while taking the Politics Class, I'd already learned to administer shots, open abscesses, clean wounds, and perform other procedures that would have been covered in both the Health Worker and Nursing programs. Once I'd earned my Politics Class Certificate, and because I'd been volunteering at the hospital throughout the Politics Class, I was permitted to bypass both the Health Worker and Nursing programs offered and enroll directly in the more advanced Medic Program.

The Medic Program

The Medic Program was highly sought after by Medical Staff Volunteers. However, only six candidates were selected by its instructor, Mary Beth Brown. I was one of them. Because of this, some were jealous of me and didn't like me. I was quite skinny and malnourished, and I was made fun of. Others would say, *"You better be careful or you're going to fall over carrying all of those schoolbooks!"*

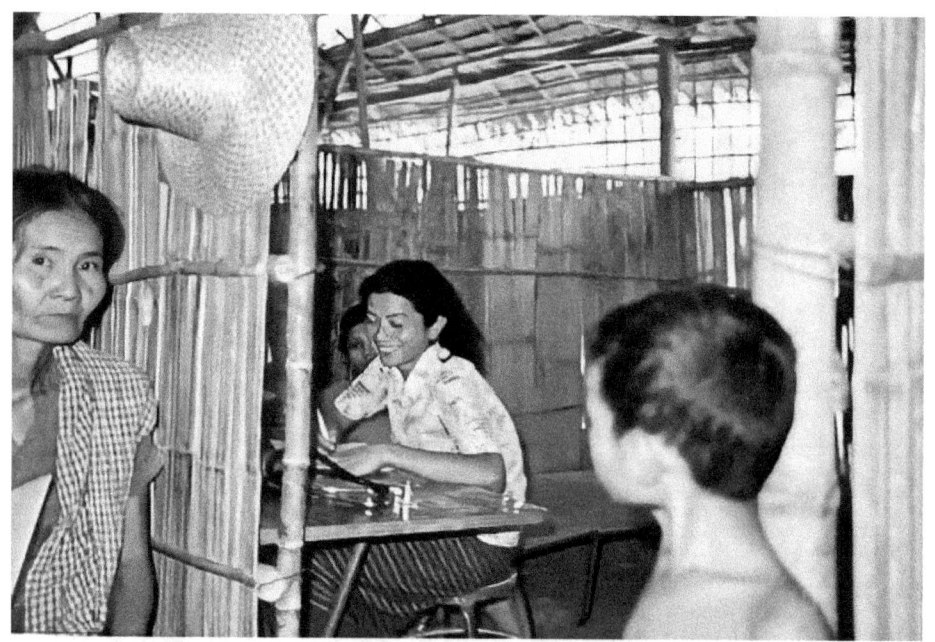

Veera collecting patient history at Site 2 Camp. *Photo credit: Veera Som.*

Each morning, I studied, then worked in the afternoons doing the procedures I was learning about in school. Not only was I learning how to be a medic, but I was simultaneously learning to both read and write in the English language. I wasn't paid for the work that I did at the hospital. I was strictly a volunteer. I was content to earn an education in the medical field and to serve others. There were fringe benefits that came with being a student and volunteer hospital worker. I earned a hospital-assigned food card in addition to the one that all women received in camp, which provided me with additional food for my household. I also received kerosene for the lantern for our home, which enabled me to study at home after dark.

I continued to have flare-ups of my asthma and was hospitalized because of it. There were times when I was taken by ambulance to the Khao I Dang Refugee Camp Hospital in Thailand because they had oxygen and Rithysen did not. ARC paid the expenses.

Developing Friendships with the American Refugee Committee (ARC) Staff

Mary Beth Brown and I became friends. As I said earlier, she was an instructor. She didn't practice medicine at the hospital. I also became friends with Jeff Nelson and Monica Overkamp. Jeff would sometimes buy meals in town and was so kind to share them with me. What a special treat that was. Jeff was a kind man. He would check on me when I was hospitalized at Khao I Dang. I appreciated the support my American friends gave me. The American ARC staff worked at the hospital for periods of approximately six to twelve months, then they'd return to the United States. Sometimes they would return. I just hated seeing them go when it came time for them to leave.

Full-time Medic Staff Volunteer

I completed the Medic Program and worked full-time as a medic in the Out-Patient Department (OPD). In addition, I worked a few nights each week at the ARC Hospital, rotating between its four wards: the Adult Ward, the Pediatrics Ward, the Ob-Gyn Ward, and the Tuberculosis (TB) Clinic. The TB Clinic was extremely busy. During the night shift, staff took turns sleeping. When we were very busy, nobody got much sleep.

The Obstetrics and Gynecology Program

Following the completion of my medic course, I was selected to participate in the Obstetrics and Gynecology Program. I had a very busy schedule. I spent the majority of my time either in the classroom or at the hospital. I moved from my cousin Kim Sur's home to an elderly couple's home that was also located close by the hospital. I had more time to study living there. Initially, the couple I lived with was happy to have me. I shared additional food items with them from the extra food card I earned as a hospital worker, as well as gifts of food that I received from my American friends.

I began caring for new arrivals from my village who traveled to the border seeking medical services from the ARC Hospital. This was a fortuitous assignment for me. In my conversations with these patients, I'd hear much-welcome news from my village and from my family. My patients served as messengers from my family and, once they returned home again, passed along messages to my family from me as well. It was so good to be in communication with my family back home again.

I enjoyed the work I was doing at the ARC Hospital and taking care of the sick. It was rewarding to provide them with whatever means of comfort I could. At times I became disheartened by some of my fellow Cambodian hospital volunteers. During the night shift, when no American supervisors were on duty, I witnessed Cambodian nurse and medic volunteers stealing medication. Their motivation was to sell it on the black market in camp. For example, one of my patients was prescribed an IV for a 24-hour period, he was to receive 3 liters of IV fluid. A Cambodian colleague of mine slowed down the IV drip to save the unused portion, then stole the IV solution and sold it on the black market. Another problem that ARC had was with some Cambodian hospital volunteers writing bad prescriptions. Because of this, American ARC supervisors found it necessary to closely monitor some employees. However, I was honest and ethical. I earned a reputation among my American colleagues as an honest, hardworking staff volunteer who provided exceptional patient care.

1984

It was now 1984, and I'd been living and working in Rithysen Camp since late 1982. I was working in the Ob-Gyn Ward as an obstetrician, gynecologist, and medic. Not all of the Cambodian volunteers were trained or skilled enough to serve in all these disciplines. When complications arose during patient care, I was often the one called upon. For instance, a woman who was in her first trimester of pregnancy was diagnosed with tuberculosis. I was responsible for calling a conference with the American medical staff, who would then determine the course of care for her. Another time, a neighbor of mine from my home village was admitted to the Adult Ward where I was working, with a distended stomach. We treated him with a diuretic (water pill) to increase his urination. When new patients arrived at the border, like my neighbor, they were given two meals per day—one in the morning and one at lunch. These travelers were provided with no evening meal. I began providing them with an evening meal that I brought from home. I was able to serve many people this way. At home, I'd been asking the elderly couple I lived with for an extra bowl of soup or rice, which I then shared with these hospital patients. Because of the extra rations I received for being a volunteer hospital staff person, I was providing extra food at home, so I didn't feel that I was taking away from what belonged to the elderly couple. But over time, the elderly couple grew unhappy about my practice of food sharing.

In the meantime, my sister Channy, while living in my father's home, had begun hearing news of me from patients I'd treated from my village and from smugglers who traveled back and forth. Channy now knew where I was living and working and that I was doing well.

My Sister Channy Arrives at Rithysen Resettlement Camp

One day in 1984, Channy arrived at camp and surprised me at the hospital. It was wonderful to see her and to be together with family again. I requested that the chief of the quarter register Channy at camp. Together we requested the materials the camp provided to build a home for us to share. Channy was here to stay! Our father had permitted her to come. He thought it would be good for us to be together. Friends of mine from camp built the shelter for us. We were happy to have our own home. Channy was eager to study to become a health care worker. Soon Channy was accepted into the Health Care Worker Program and began volunteer work at the ARC Hospital. She wasn't required to take the Politics Class. Once she completed the Health Care Worker Program, she then completed the OB class. When Channy had completed her studies, we began working together in obstetrics and delivered many babies.

Five people sitting in a circle on bamboo bed at Site 2 Camp; Veera with Spoon and Channy blue shirt. *Photo credit: Veera Som.*

Many of our patients suffered from a variety of STDs. I examined them, sent samples to the lab for testing, and prescribed medications to treat both my patients and their sexual partners. It was difficult to control the STD outbreak in camp. Many men had numerous sexual partners. As their health care workers, we would advocate to our women patients that we wanted to not only treat them but their partners as well and that they should request that their sexual partners come to be tested too. One of my patients went home and reported to her partner that she had gonorrhea. She explained to him that the medical providers requested that he be tested and treated as well. A sexual partner may also have an STD but may not yet be symptomatic. This patient's husband became enraged. He hastily arrived at the hospital threatening staff while carrying a hand grenade. *"How dare the hospital staff insinuate that he has gonorrhea."* The hospital was quickly evacuated. Thankfully, he did not detonate the hand grenade.

I had a suitor at Rithysen Camp. I met Touch (sounds like *tewk)* at Politics Class, where we soon became friends. He liked visiting me at the hospital and at my home. He fell in love with me. Touch sent his mother to see me, and she requested my permission for her son to marry me. I told his mother no, that I did not want to marry anyone while living in the camp. Touch was embarrassed following my refusal of his proposal and kept his distance from me after that.

ARC staff women at Rithysen Camp. *Photo credit: Veera Som.*

1985—The Vietnamese Army Destroyed Rithysen Camp Overnight

One evening in early 1985, I was working night duty in OB. I'd been working especially hard delivering babies and attending to women in various stages of labor. About 2:00 a.m. the sounds of shelling by the Vietnamese army could be heard exploding in the distance. This wasn't unusual. But then the noise grew closer and closer until it was literally occurring in camp, just outside the hospital. There was nothing we could do but run. Tragically, I had to leave a patient who was crowning and ready to deliver her baby. Those who could run—our pregnant patients in labor, my fellow medical colleagues, and I—ran for our lives. We ran for nearly five hours before arriving at the Cambodia–Thailand border. Thai guards were there guarding the border and prohibited any passage into Thailand. Thai soldiers fought back the Vietnamese with their shelling from a large cannon. All of us camp evacuees were caught in the midst of the fighting. My patients in labor, my hospital colleagues and I, and the rest of the evacuees from Rithysen Camp could only keep our heads down to the ground and wait for the shelling to stop. I watched while Thai soldiers were literally shooting over us, fighting to keep the Vietnamese soldiers from crossing into Thailand.

When morning came, the shelling had ended. About 45,000 of us evacuated Rithysen Camp and gathered at the border crossing. All of us were now up on our feet and in desperate search to reunite with our loved ones.

Normally, when I worked on night duty, so did my sister, but that night Channy had remained at home. While living at border camps under the constant threat of shelling around us, it was common practice to pack every night in case of a sudden evacuation. We'd cook rice and dry it in the sunshine during the daytime. At night we would pack the dry rice with the intention that water could be added on the run to eat later. Also, fish, tuna, and snacks would be made ready. These items would be wrapped in a krama (scarf), basket, or whatever we might have. Medicine would also be packed, along with any essential items. These packs would then be available to grab at a minute's notice if it became time to flee. Everybody did the same thing. Families with children were prepared with a plan for who would carry what. This was how we lived during wartime.

It is impossible to express in words how elated I was to find my sister Channy. I studied her up and down to make certain she was okay. She had encountered an explosion while fleeing from

Rithysen Camp. Her sarong was blackened and singed with burn holes. Channy wasn't even aware of it. It was a close call, but she too had escaped uninjured. Channy had fled from our home, so she carried with her our essentials: some food, my adrenaline medication that I used to control my asthma, and a few other items. We lost Rithysen Camp and our meager home, the ARC Hospital; everything had burned. Many people were killed in the blasts, but Channy and I were safe.

Rithysen Camp Relocated to a Temporary Location Known as Red Hill Camp across the Border in Thailand

Soon the ARC representatives, UNBRO (United Nation Border Release Operation), the journalists, the news media were there. Initially, the ARC team informed us that we would remain there for now to ensure our safety. Negotiations were underway with the Thai commander to permit all of us to enter Thailand. At about 12:00 noon, Thai guards opened the gates to the border and let approximately 45,000 of us displaced Cambodian people inside the country of Thailand. UNBRO provided us with provisions for food and water. It was not enough, but it was something. We walked until dusk, carrying what little belongings we had with us, and arrived at a location deemed Red Hill Camp that would be operated by the Thai Task Force. There was no camp set up. No guards were in place. We all camped under the stars and the trees that first night. People cooked the food they'd carried with them. All were exhausted from travel and slept.

The next day, a water truck arrived, and sheets of plastic were distributed for people to use to make their tents. A large tent was erected at Red Hill for the ARC Hospital. The ARC staff who I'd worked with at Rithysen Camp hadn't fled the hospital with those of us who'd been working the night shift when the blasts occurred, as they lived outside of camp and left camp every day at 5:00 p.m. These same ARC staff arrived at Red Hill Camp quickly, and once again we began treating patients, including the injured, the sick, and the women in labor. Channy and I slept at the hospital.

Khmer Resistance Army Soldiers Wreaked Havoc in Camp

I had an unrealistic sense of relief and safety initially at Red Hill Camp. I was relieved to be in Thailand and less worried about shelling because the Vietnamese army wouldn't be able to reach us inside of Thailand. This camp was still a relocation camp, not a refugee camp. However, at Red Hill Camp we were surrounded by the jungle and were now closer to the border than we were at Rithysen Camp. The border is where much of the fighting took place. There were soldiers living amongst us in Red Hill Camp. They appeared as civilians and were not dressed in their army attire, but they carried their guns. Things were quiet at camp during the daytime hours, but after the ARC employees had left for the night, the Khmer Resistance Army (KRA) soldiers embedded in camp would wreak havoc. The KRA, through their personal networks, learned who in camp carried gold and money, and they robbed and killed people every night. Gunshots, screams, and terror permeated our nights in camp. All of us were afraid and feared for our lives. After one week in camp, the UNHCR (United Nations High Commissioner for Refugees) requested permission from the Thai Task Force to move the camp occupants of Red Hill to a new and safer location within Thailand. Permission was granted.

Rithysen Camp at Red Hill Relocated to Barnng Phou Camp in Thailand, Adjacent to Khao I Dang Refugee Camp

This time we were relocated by bus to Barnng Phou Camp. The Thai Task Force carefully screened the men, looking for any possible soldiers, any uniforms, or guns. In fact, the entrance into camp for all young men was very strict and highly restricted, with most men not permitted entry. The camp population was predominantly women and children. Old men were also allowed.

Living Conditions at Barnng Phou Camp Were Poor

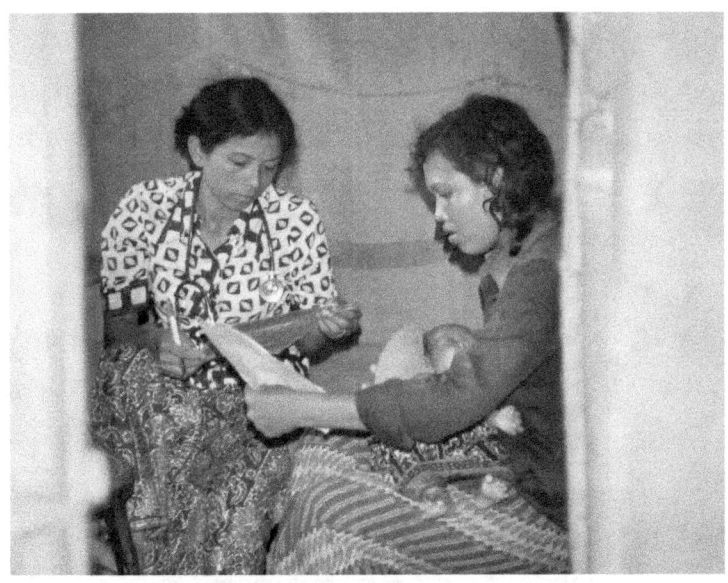

Veera with stethoscope and patients, a mom and a baby.
Photo credit: Veera Som.

I continued to work in the ARC Hospital. Barnng Phou Camp was much smaller than the camps where we'd previously lived. People's homes at this camp were built even closer together and were smaller in size. Hygienic conditions were poor. Toilets were located next to the houses, which made for very smelly conditions. Rain would fall and conditions would become extremely unsanitary and completely unacceptable. People in camp weren't able to sneak out to buy food like was done at other camps. The Thai Task Force was very strict when I lived there. There was not enough food to eat. We received only rice and canned tuna. We ate this every day. Water was delivered to camp as before, with each person provided 25 liters per day. That was not enough. As the living conditions at Barnng Phou Camp were difficult, more people were sick and, in the hospital, which made my work at the hospital very stressful. Many factors contributed to the lack of wellness at camp, including the poor hygienic conditions, and not only the shortage of food but also the absence of fruit and vegetables in our diet. We could not leave camp to forage for fresh food, nor for any reason, or we would be shot by the Thai Task Force.

Khao I Dang Refugee Camp – Where Refugees Would Either Be Repatriated to Cambodia or Expatriated to a Third Country
Barnng Phou Resettlement Camp bordered the Khao I Dang Refugee Camp (KID). Khao I Dang Refugee Camp (KID) was a Cambodian refugee camp that served as a temporary holding center for refugees who would either be repatriated to Cambodia or expatriated to third countries. Its population eventually reached 160,000. The only thing that separated the two camps was a

barbed-wire fence. People living in each camp could see one another, and some would communicate together by writing notes, attaching them to sticks, and throwing them across the fence. Those living in the refugee camp knew that people in our resettlement camp were starving. At times they would throw food to us over the fence. The refugees at Khao I Dang received more food provisions than we did at the resettlement camp. Because of this, there were people from our camp attempting to leave our camp to gain entrance to the refugee camp. With so many displaced persons at Barnng Phou Camp who would prefer to live in the refugee camp, the Thai Task Force heavily guarded it. Those attempting to enter Khao I Dang Refugee Camp illegally were warned that they would be shot. The UNHCR cautioned everybody against attempting entry into Khao I Dang.

Extremely Stressful Work Conditions at Barnng Phou Camp

My sister Channy and I continued working at the ARC Hospital at Barnng Phou Camp in the OB Department delivering babies. Staff were so incredibly busy at this camp. We'd become exhausted. Some would call in sick, which would exacerbate the hardship because we'd have even less staff. I wasn't one to call in sick. One day I was working quite sleep-deprived, I admit. I was assisting a woman in labor who was delivering her second child. The conditions of her delivery weren't ideal. The surface she was lying on was uneven, and the patient was moving a lot. She became hysterical in labor. When she pushed the baby out, she experienced a second-degree tear of her perineum. My supervisor, an ARC staff person from Belgium, became irate that this had happened and publicly blamed me in front of the patient and her family. She then sent me home. This upset me. My supervisor demonstrated no compassion for the challenging work conditions. She was too quick to place blame. For a number of days, I chose to stay home and did not return to work. Frankly, I'd been humiliated and didn't want to return to OB under her supervision. But I did miss my work. When the unit got terribly busy yet again, this supervisor paid me a visit at home and apologized. She wanted me back, but I said no. Not prepared to take no for an answer, she sent another ARC staff person, my teacher and friend Mary Beth Brown, to speak with me. Mary Beth encouraged me to return to OB. I tried to negotiate a reassignment with her to either the Adult or Pediatrics wards, but Mary Beth was firm in her request, pleading that OB really needed me. I was trained as both a medic and a midwife, and my skills were needed there. Men were not allowed to deliver babies in Cambodia, which exacerbated the situation. I agreed to return to OB. My supervisor and I developed a good working relationship after that. There were joyful moments with every new birth. The ARC Hospital gifted each mom a new sarong following their deliveries, and each baby received a newborn outfit gifted by my supervisor. Channy delivered about 300 babies while working in the ARC OB, and I delivered approximately 50 babies. Overall, I'd worked primarily in GYN, not OB.

Rithysen Camp at Barnng Phou Camp in Thailand Relocated to Site 2 Camp Located Next to the Dangrek Mountain in Cambodia

After seven months' time in Barnng Phou Camp, the border fighting had quieted. All of us displaced persons living here were relocated to a camp at the border called Site 2 Camp, located next to the Dangrek Mountain, where one side of the mountain was Cambodia and the other, Thailand. Site 2 was surrounded by a jungle. Prior to our arrival, the UNHCR cleared the site of trees. Once again, it was the job of those of us displaced to set up the camp and put up the houses. This relocation was a major undertaking. An ARC Hospital tent was erected. Channy and I shared a small house built for us by friends. Soon we were back again working in the ARC Hospital and had resumed a familiar routine.

At this point in time, Channy and I had resettled in four resettlement camps: 1) Rithysen Khmer Resettlement Camp in Cambodia (1982–1984); 2) Rithysen Camp located at Red Hill Camp in Thailand (early 1985 for just a few weeks); 3) Barnng Phou Camp in Thailand (approx. 7 months); and 4) Site 2 Camp by Dangrek Mountain, Cambodia

After some time living at Site 2 Camp, Channy and I began serious discussions about how to escape from Site 2 Camp and then illegally enter into the Khao I Dang Refugee Camp. We had both grown weary of all the moving from camp to camp; we didn't wish to return to Cambodia; and we both were dreaming of one day immigrating to a third country. Site 2 Camp wasn't a safe place to live, nor did it provide us with an opportunity to immigrate to a third country since it was a resettlement camp, not a refugee camp.

1986

ARC staff Jeff Nelson and others and Veera doing a training exercise at Site 2 Camp. *Photo credit: Veera Som.*

In early 1986 I confided with Jeff Nelson of our scheming, one of our closest friends from ARC, and a few other ARC friends. In his work, Jeff transported ambulance patients between Site 2 Camp and Khao I Dang Refugee Camp. Of course, nobody liked our plans or wanted us to leave, as they worried about our safety. They suggested that at some point down the line, the refugee camp would open up to new occupants again and that we'd have an opportunity to apply for a ration card then and enter the refugee camp legally. Channy and I did not want to wait. After living and working in Site 2 Camp for a number of months, we began putting our plans in motion. Vanna, a Cambodian colleague of ours who was also an ARC volunteer like us, had connections within the Khao I Dang Refugee Camp. He agreed to make plans to escort us illegally for a fee. We were offered two choices for traveling to Khao I Dang: one was by car and the other was on foot. We would have two guides and understood that going by car would be a more expensive option. Our plan was put into place. Channy, Paul (a coworker), and Sarin would go first with the two guides on foot. After they'd safely arrived at Khao I Dang Refugee Camp, I would follow with Paul's mom and our two guides by car.

Veera holding a bouquet of flowers with ARC staff members at Site 2 Camp. *Photo credit: Veera Som.*

Escape from Site 2 Camp and Illegal Entry to Khao I Dang Refugee Camp

Once Channy and her group had successfully arrived at Khao I Dang, Vanna delivered a note from Channy through our guide, who travels between the two camps, that Paul's mom and I should start out. Vanna and I secured our plans for departure, I confided in a few trusted ARC friends, and we were ready to go. Vanna, a second guide, Paul's mom, and I left Site 2 Camp on foot in the evening after dark. Vanna spoke Cambodian and Thai, and our other guide spoke only Thai. We walked for a while, and then Thai soldiers began shooting at us. Paul's mom and I took refuge in the cornfield. Our two guides approached the Thai soldiers and offered them a bribe, and the soldiers allowed us to continue on. Vanna came looking for us and found Paul's mom and me terrified and lying flat on the ground, hiding in the cornfield. We resumed walking. There was no road, only a jungle. My companion and I kept expecting to come upon a car because we had paid for car transportation, but regardless, we continued on foot a long way in the dark. We waded through increasingly deeper water until it reached my chin. I didn't know how to swim, so I reached out and grabbed our second guide, who was in my lead. He slapped me across the face. He mistakenly thought I was grabbing for his gun, and he didn't understand what I was saying because he spoke only Thai. I tried to communicate with Vanna, but he was too far ahead of me. We stayed silent to avoid drawing attention to ourselves. I couldn't call out to him. Fortunately, the water leveled off and did not get any deeper. Soon we emerged onto dry land. Up ahead of us on the road, a pickup truck was waiting. It was nearly 5:00 a.m.

Paul's mom and I and one of our guides jumped into the back of the pickup. Vanna sat up in front with the driver, and we traveled 10 or 15 minutes by truck before we were dropped off to continue on foot. After a short walk, we reached Khao I Dang Camp. As we approached the spiraled barbed-wire fence, our Thai-speaking guide stretched and lifted the barbed wire up, and we crawled under it and onto the other side. We were now inside the Khao I Dang Refugee Camp. The armed Thai guards were there waiting.

Our guides paid the Thai guards bribes, and we were permitted to pass and walk into camp. It was early morning. All was still dark and quiet. Our guides led us to a house where a woman inside was expecting us. She welcomed us in. We laid down on a bamboo bed and slept until daylight.

CHAPTER 4

KHAO I DANG REFUGEE CAMP – ILLEGAL RESIDENTS

That morning Vanna took us to see Channy, Paul, and Sarin. We learned that the Thai Task Force was actively working to identify illegals in camp. The homeowners, Virak and Sarom, were taking a chance by providing us with shelter. The five of us illegals stayed with them for a month or two. We didn't dare go anywhere. We just remained at the house day and night. Then an announcement was broadcast throughout camp that if illegals were apprehended, both the illegals and the hosts harboring them would be jailed and sent back to the border. Although unspoken, we were all becoming more fearful of being discovered. Channy, Sarin, and I appreciated the risks that Virak and Sarin were taking by allowing us to stay in their home. We didn't know what difficulties they'd already experienced while seeking their ration cards, but we decided to leave their home so as not to put them in further jeopardy.

Making the MSF Hospital Our Home Base

Khao I Dang Refugee Camp, in front of the French Doctors Without Borders Hospital. *Photo credit: Veera Som.*

Our new plan was to explore the viability of settling in at the MSF Hospital in camp. The camp hospital was operated by a French organization, not ARC (American Refugee Committee). We kept our eyes out for our friend Jeff Nelson, who was in and out of the MSF Hospital shuttling patients back and forth from Site 2 Camp. We were delighted when we finally spotted each other. He gifted us some cooked Thai food that was delicious and generously gave us some cash. We confided to Jeff that we were now going to try to make the hospital our home base. Hospital staff weren't only treating legal residents of Khao I Dang. It appeared to us that they didn't make it their business to know who among them were illegals.

Channy, Sarin, and I made our way into the hospital. Channy and I began lingering in the Lactation Room. Mothers of infants expressed their breast milk here and shared their milk with babies who had none. Before long, we were assisting these patients. Food service was provided three times daily for the hospital patients. Channy and I each had a bowl and spoon, and we followed along with the food servers, hoping that there would be enough food for us. Sometimes there was other times there was not. We began sleeping in the Lactation Room. Unlike the ARC Hospital, MSF Hospital staff slept at the hospital overnight. Paul and his mother stayed at their relatives' home, who were legal refugees. Sarin also stayed at the hospital.

TTF (Thai Task Force) Search for Illegals

More and more illegals were doing the same thing. It became apparent that the Thai Task Force (TTF) knew that many illegals were staying in the building. One night the TTF came to catch the illegals. About 10:00 p.m. the Thai Task Force's car was spotted outside the hospital. A Cambodian staff person working in the Pediatrics Unit gave everybody a heads-up that the TTF would be conducting a search for illegals. We had about thirty minutes before they arrived.

We felt trapped and quickly needed to come up with a plan to avoid them. We were part of a group of seven illegals. We decided to take cover in the attic space, just above the bamboo ceiling. A couple of the men climbed up and opened the ceiling. We took turns climbing the bamboo walls and hid there in the attic. Once we were all tucked up above the bamboo ceiling, the opening was sealed up. In our haste, we forgot to carry our shoes with us, and they were left behind. Hospital staff kindly gathered our shoes and hid them. Here I was in this dusty attic, and I had severe asthma. I needed to sneeze very badly. Soon the Thai Task Force entered the Lactating Room. We could see them below. They carried flashlights and shined them up to the ceiling. We were very quiet and held our breath. I held my sneezes. Much to our amazement, they did not detect us above the ceiling, and they moved on. We all stayed put until hospital staff notified us that the TTF had gone. My heart had been pounding so hard in my chest. I thought for certain that they'd find us and that we'd be put in jail. But that didn't happen. Instead, we climbed back down and slept there until morning. Again, it was time to come up with a new plan.

Our Safe House with Tunnel for Sleeping was Located in Section 21 of Khao I Dang

A man named Sung, who Channy and I knew from our home village, was aware of our situation. He was a legal resident of Khao I Dang and had a house in camp but was not living there. Sung graciously offered us refuge in his home. Because the Thai Task Force was searching for illegals, we created a few safety measures inside the house. We added a false wall parallel to the shared wall with our neighbors. Between the false wall and shared wall, we dug a tunnel where the three of us could sleep. We retired to this tunnel every night. We couldn't completely stretch our bodies out, but we could lie in a relaxed fetal position, end to end. Because of my asthma, I coveted the position closest to the entrance, where I breathed easier. We hollowed out a bamboo pole and placed it with one end outside the tunnel and one end inside, to provide an oxygen source. The tunnel was wide enough so that if the furthest person inside the tunnel wanted to, they could crawl out and the other two could remain in place. We kept a candle inside and burned it for light. We shared our sleeping tunnel with cockroaches and other insects. It was muddy and oftentimes wet. Once the three of us were in the tunnel for the night, we would scrape dirt from the surface over the entrance and pull a bamboo mat over the dirt to conceal the entrance hole. Sometimes friends would cover us up. Oftentimes, we didn't remain inside the tunnel all night long because it was difficult to breathe. We emerged from the tunnel muddy each and every day.

Veera and Channy sitting in sleeping/hiding tunnel.
Photo credit: Veera Som.

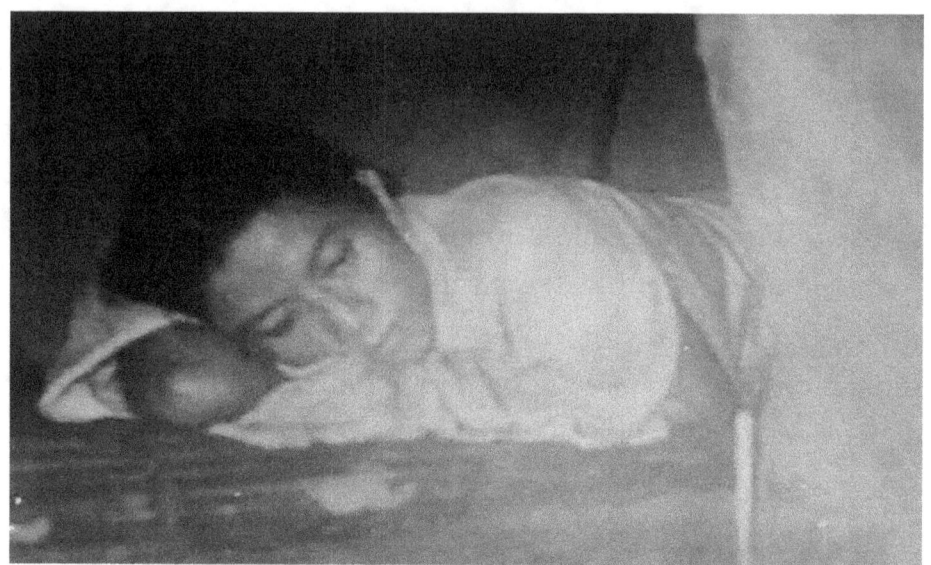

Veera resting in the tunnel they hid in from the Thai Task Force overnight.
Photo credit: Veera Som.

Hiding in Plain Sight – Friends and Colleagues Looked Out for Veera and Channy

Our house was located in Section 21 of Khao I Dang. Section 21 had many long-term refugees, some living there since 1979, who hadn't successfully completed immigration interviews for a third country. These people had no qualms about hiding illegals. We became friends with our neighbors. It was imperative that we had good relationships with them to avoid someone turning us in. My sister and I helped out a family of seven with their daily chores and they kept us fed. They looked out for us and would alert us when the Thai Task Force vehicle was in camp. Others who knew that we were illegals invited us to their homes and would share their food with us, but we avoided letting anybody know where we lived. At night, the chief of the quarter, who was in charge of food and provisions, watched out for us too. Because we were illegals, we couldn't get a ration card. Without the help of others, we would have had nothing to eat. We lived in this house for a year and a half, sleeping in the tunnel nearly every night and receiving handouts for our food.

Babysat neighbors' kids at Khao I. Dang Refugee Camp. Parents helped provide us with food and assisted us in hiding. *Photo credit: Veera Som.*

Working in the OPD (Outpatient Department) in Khao I Dang Refugee Camp

We had other kind people who looked out for us as well. My former colleague and friend from ARC, Dr. Pat Walker, knew someone who worked at OPD (the Outpatient Department) and learned that they needed help in Gynecology. Despite the fact that they knew I was living in Camp Khao I Dang illegally, they hired me because of my support from Dr. Walker. I worked there for three months. I didn't earn money, but they provided me with food rations of rice, salt, and sometimes sugar, and while working there I had easy access to medicine when I needed it. I had to be very careful walking to and from the OPD and weaved in and out between the houses, never walking on the main road. While at the OPD, it was necessary for me to remain in the patient care room at all times. After a while, a male staff person in the OPD began asking questions about my legal status and where I lived. Because I no longer felt safe there and didn't want to cause trouble for those who'd been watching out for me, I quit my job.

One of my friends from the ARC Resettlement Camp Hospital was Jean Jachman. She was a nurse and would provide me with inhalers while we were working together, for which I was extremely grateful. Later, when I was living in Khao I Dang, she was back in Minnesota. *[Jean ended up sponsoring Virak and Sarom, the couple we first stayed with at Khao I Dang.]*

My ARC Friends and Colleagues Explored Options for Me to Immigrate to the US as a Humanitarian Parolee (HP) Due to My Severe Asthma

Jeff Nelson, Monica Overkamp, and Jean Jachman became my benefactors. I was friends with each of them. We worked together as colleagues in resettlement camps. I believe they appreciated my strong work ethic and honesty. Because of my asthma, each of them feared for my health. Unbeknownst to me, they began to collectively explore options for me to immigrate to the United States. Because I was not a legal refugee, nor did I have any family already living in the US, they looked into my coming to the US as a humanitarian parolee (HP) case. Jean Jachman, who was in the US at that time, contacted Glenda Potter, a Minnesota immigration lawyer, on my behalf. She discussed my case with her. In the meantime, Jeff Nelson was in and out of Khao I Dang and kept current on my situation in camp. Glenda Potter agreed to take on my case and made plans to fly to Thailand to meet with me.

Celebration for woman (far right) who was approved for immigration to a third country; Veera in blue, Channy in pink. *Photo credit: Veera Som.*

I met with Dr. Walker who informed me of the plans that were underway. She said Glenda Potter, the immigration lawyer from the United State who lived in the state of Minnesota would be flying to Cambodia to meet with me. Glenda would attempt to help Channy and me immigrate to the United States. Wow. I felt so privileged and special that an American woman would be coming all the way from the United States just to meet with me. I was extremely excited to receive this news from Dr. Pat Walker.

The three Walker sisters in Thailand in 1988. Left to right Elizabeth
Walker Anderson, Pat Walker and Susan Walker.
Photo credit: Dr. Walker.

Meeting Glenda Potter, US Immigration Lawyer

And then Glenda Potter came. It was in early 1988. She arrived at
our door in Section 21 of Khao I Dang. Glenda was wearing a
white blouse and a blue skirt, not unlike the uniform I wore to
school in my childhood so many years before. I was amazed that
she had arrived. She was an angel who had come to rescue me.
We invited her in. Glenda took a seat on the bamboo bed, the
only piece of furniture we had, and she began interviewing us.
She completed some forms -- filled in our names, how long we
were at camp, and asked many questions relating to my history
with asthma. Glenda said that she learned of my story through
Jean Jachman and that they were all trying to help get me to the
United States, but that she couldn't promise me anything yet. My
asthma was going to be a critical factor in my eligibility for my
immigration.

Veera, Channy and Glenda Potter, Immigration Lawyer.
Photo credit: Veera Som.

Glenda instructed me to contact all the doctors I'd worked with and known throughout the years in the resettlement camps, as well as in Khao I Dang Refugee Camp, and request each of them to write a letter of support, speaking to my health history of asthma. Glenda wanted me to be sure to convey to my medical references what my asthma triggers were and what circumstances while in the camps most exacerbated my asthma. Once I'd completed my outreach and received their letters of recommendation, Glenda directed me to transmit them to Jeff Nelson.

I got started. Dr. Pat Walker, Monica Overkamp, and Jean Jachman had already written their letters on my behalf. Doctors from Khao I Dang also wrote letters. Jeff assisted me in reaching out to the doctors I'd worked with at the resettlement camps and was kind enough to collect those letters for me. These were prominent people that I highly respected. I was honored to receive their support. Jean Jachman, my nurse friend, whose husband was a commercial airline pilot for Northwest Airlines in America; Monica Overkamp, whose husband Mark was a kidney specialist at the University of Minnesota; and Betty Mitchell, a physician's assistant I worked with at Rithysen Camp, who resided in Hawaii, also wrote letters. I am eternally grateful to these people, for their friendship, and their resolve to assist me with my immigration.

Monica Overkamp
Photo credit: Veera Som.

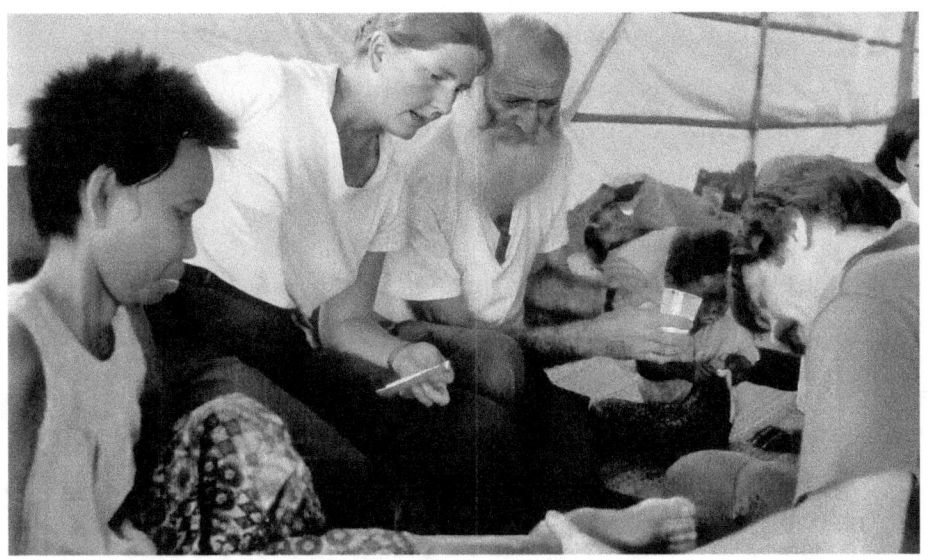
Dr. Walker with leprosy patient. *Photo credit: Dr. Walker.*

My Four Sponsors

I was required to have four sponsors, and they were: Jeff Nelson, Betty Mitchell, Glenda Potter, and Jean Jachman. There was an initial plan for me to live in Hawaii, but this plan was ruled out because of concern that my asthma might react to the volcanic air there. Glenda Potter subsequently agreed to host me in Minnesota, and provide for my housing and food. My other sponsors would provide financial support. Because I was unsuccessful at gaining legal refugee status at Khao I Dang, the US federal government would not cover my immigration expenses.

Immigration and Naturalization Interviews for Me and Channy

Three months following my initial meeting with Glenda Potter, she notified me that I had an interview scheduled with Immigration. She explained, however, that Immigration could not conduct their interviews with me and Channy at Khao I Dang because we were not living there legally. The time had come for Channy and me to return to Site 2 Camp. During this entire immigration discussion process, Glenda made it clear to me that Channy was a part of my immigration case. However, Glenda stated that she could not guarantee Channy's acceptance by the Immigration and Naturalization Services (INS), I understood, but I was adamant that I would not go without my sister. In the end, Glenda wrote a very compelling letter on behalf of Channy, and this letter was submitted with my application.

Turned Ourselves in as Illegals at the Thai Task Force Office in Khao I Dang Refugee Camp

I turned myself in as an illegal at the TTF (Thai Task Force) office in Khao I Dang, and so did Channy and Sarin. We asked to return to the Site 2 Resettlement Camp. The three of us were then added to a list of other illegals in camp that would soon be transported to Site 2. If the TTF had discovered us to be illegals on their own we would have been placed in jail and sent back to the border. But, at this time, numerous announcements were being made in camp over the intercom system that those illegals who turned themselves in would not be penalized, so we were not at risk.

Returned to Site 2 Camp in Cambodia

Ironically, a Thai Task Force vehicle, one of the same TTF vehicles we'd been fearing and so cautiously avoiding for one and a half years, chauffeured us to Site 2 Camp, upon our request. When we arrived at Site 2 Camp, we were met by the camp chief who presented us with paperwork to complete. The chief and I had known one another when I lived there. He said to me, *"Where have you been?"*

At this point, Channy and I weren't sure what to do. We had no home at Site 2 Camp. It would be another month before we had our immigration interview. We decided to ask a friend of mine who was a quarter chief, if we could stay with him, his wife, and family. Fortunately, they welcomed us to stay with them. The quarter chief registered me and my sister as residents of the quarter. This made us eligible to receive food rations. We were added as newcomers. A few months later, it was time for our interviews.

Our Final Interview with Immigration at the American Embassy in Aranyaprathet.

I received a letter from the ARC staff telling us where to catch the Thai Bus to Aranyaprathet, where the American Embassy was located, and where our interviews were to take place. We were quite worried and anxious about the interview because it would be the determining factor as to whether we were eligible to immigrate to the United States or not. I especially worried about my sister Channy—whether the two of us would be considered as one case, or, in the end, whether they would consider her application separately. Two immigration officers conducted our interviews jointly. This took most of the morning. I was so nervous my heart was practically beating out of my chest. At the conclusion of our interview, one of the immigration officers announced then and there that both of us had been accepted to immigrate to the United States. Channy and I were so relieved and thrilled with the good news. We would be notified by letter when it was time for us to leave Site 2 for Phanat Nikhom Refugee Camp.

Time to Leave Site 2 Camp and Make Our Way to Phanat Nikhom Refugee Camp

When we returned from our immigration interview to Site 2 Camp we kept our news extremely quiet and only shared it with a few select friends. We anticipated that if news spread about our imminent immigration, there might be jealousy in camp. We didn't want to take any unnecessary risks that could jeopardize our upcoming plans. We faced an uncertain timeline. As we weren't working, we stayed in the house as much as we could. Then, a few nights after being approved, we woke up to the sounds of shelling taking place close by camp. I wondered if our plans to immigrate were just too good to be true? I was doubtful of our chances to successfully leave the country. I prayed to the Buddha, asking Him to please help us to get out of the camp successfully. We were so close. With the shelling occurring all around us, camp residents left our houses and were forced to take cover in the ditches. After a few hours had passed, the bombing calmed down. Our camp was spared.

A month later, we were notified that it was time to go to Phanat Nikhom Refugee Camp that served as a processing and transit center for those destined for resettlement in third countries. Channy and I boarded the bus. We made no announcement that we were leaving, not to the ARC staff, not to anybody. It wasn't until after we were settled in at Phanat Nikhom Camp that our few trusted confidants at Site 2 Camp told the others at camp where we had gone. I'm sure they were very surprised that

I, who was pretty quiet and unassuming, had the ability to make this happen. Nobody could have been more surprised than me.

When we arrived in Phanat Nikhom, Immigration had a place ready for us to stay, along with other refugees who were also being processed for immigration. There was no war going on in this city. We were free to come and go as we pleased. Jeff Nelson had given us money for our journey, and we enjoyed going to the market to purchase delicious Thai food and other things. It had been a long time since we had such a privilege, and for that we were extremely grateful.

Physical Exams

In the meantime, we awaited our physical exams, and of course, worried whether the status our physical health would be approved. Tuberculosis was rather commonplace in camp, and if we were diagnosed with that, our plans would be put on hold as treatment for TB took nine months. People testing positive for HIV were rejected, and any hopes of immigration would be dashed. In addition, those testing positive with neurological issues were also denied. We both had our physical exams, and our results were approved for immigration.

Awaiting a Mandatory Physician Escort

At this point, there remained just one more steppingstone ahead of us, and that was to await the availability of a physician to escort us to the United States. A medical doctor's escort was a requirement for immigrating as a humanitarian parolee (HP). Six weeks later, a female physician in Bangkok became available to be our escort.

CHAPTER 5

IMMIGRATION TO THE USA FEBRUARY 1989 DEPARTURE FROM BANGKOK

Channy and I boarded the first available bus to Bangkok, the capital city of Thailand. There we met our physician escort. Our friend, Jeff Nelson with the American Refugee Committee, also met up with us there. Jeff was present to be of service to us. He prepped us on what to expect when arriving in the US. His counseling was in addition to training we had received at the Phanat Nikhom Camp about typical living conditions, federal and local laws, education, and a little bit of everything that we could expect to find when settling in the US. Channy and I were taken under everybody's wings. Our needs were taken care of for us. Jeff provided us with travel money and wished us well on our journey.

Flight from Bangkok, Thailand to the USA

The time had come. Channy and I boarded our flight along with my physician escort. We were en-route from Bangkok, Thailand, to the United States of America.

This was the first time that both Channy and I had flown. I had some difficulty on the flight. I suffered from nosebleeds as well as a severe migraine that triggered vomiting. I was extremely fortunate to be looked after by my physician escort. She took good care of me and got a flight attendant to switch my seat to a location where I was able to fully recline. The reclined position helped to alleviate my nosebleeds. We landed in San Francisco initially for a short layover before continuing on to Minnesota.

Arrival at the Minneapolis Saint Paul (MSP) International Airport, Tuesday, February 21, 1989

Veera and Channy's smiles MSP Airport, Minnesota, 2/21/1989.
Photo credit: Veera Som.

Veera and Channy's Arrival at MSP Airport, Minnesota 2/21/1989. *Photo credit: Veera Som.*

We arrived on Tuesday, February 21, 1989, in the late afternoon on the day after our departure from Bangkok at the Minneapolis Saint Paul International Airport (MSP). As the airplane taxied in for a landing, my physician escort told me to look out the small airplane window. Everything was covered in a blanket of white. It was something I'd never seen before. *"What am I seeing?"* I asked. She just smiled and said, *"It's snow, Veera. It's winter in Minnesota and it's cold!"*

My physician escort accompanied us as we deplaned. Glenda Potter greeted us at our gate. She was accompanied by Dr. Pat Walker from the American Refugee Committee (ARC), a local news reporter from WCCO News, and about fifteen others. I was still feeling quite poorly, but that aside, there was much excitement surrounding us. A friend of Glenda's handed a winter jacket to each of us. I wasn't cold and didn't think I needed it, but

Glenda assured me, *"You're going to need the jacket Veera! It may be warm inside the airport but the temperature outside is cold!"*

Local Television News, WCCO Interview

Tuesday, February 21, 1989. This was the day we arrived in Minnesota. There was a twelve-hour time difference between Bangkok, Thailand, and Minneapolis, Minnesota. We had just flown over 8,200 miles to get here. Everything we were experiencing here at the MSP Airport felt surreal to me and Channy, and then a reporter from WCCO, a local news station, and her camera crew, approached us and requested an interview. The reporter asked, *"How do you feel now that you're here in the United States?"*

"I feel so happy and relieved!" I responded. Yet, many mixed feelings were flooding through my mind: *"How am I going to live in this country?"* I thought to myself. I literally felt as though I was floating through clouds as if in a daydream. There was so very much to process. It was an out-of-body experience.

My physician escort bid us farewell. We picked up our simple pieces of luggage at Baggage Claim. As you'd expect, we carried very little with us: a few changes of clothing, a few personal items, and then there was one luxury item that I'd brought along all the way from Thailand—a sack of sugar.

EPILOGUE

OUR HOMECOMING—TUESDAY, FEBRUARY 21, 1989

From the airport Glenda drove us to her home, our new home in Eagan, Minnesota. A party awaited us there with about fifteen in attendance. Jean Jachman and Dr. Pat Walker, both from ARC, were present, along with Glenda's friend Kim and a number of Cambodian immigrants. Upon entering Glenda's house there were so many things that were brand new to us. The first thing I asked about was the light-colored carpet on the floor. I'd never seen carpet and was very curious how Glenda kept it clean. Earlier that day Glenda's Cambodian friends gathered here and cooked Cambodian food for our Welcome Home Celebration. An entire buffet was awaiting us when we arrived. They made egg rolls, fried rice, and an Asian salad. The telephone rang. American Refugee Committee (ARC) staff were calling to welcome us to Minnesota. Glenda called to us, *"Pick up the phone!"* We had not used a telephone before! Glenda was delighted to welcome us to her home. She was smiling from ear to ear. She had comfortable beds made up for us to sleep in. We had never slept on anything that comfortable in our entire lives.

The next day Channy and I opened Glenda's kitchen cupboards and were surprised and delighted to discover that they were stocked with the staples that we had back home in Cambodia. Glenda's friend Thaly had gone Asian food shopping for us in advance of our arrival and had stocked Glenda's kitchen with fish sauce, soy sauce, garlic, galanga (ginger), and rice. Our kitchen was equipped for us to start cooking for ourselves from day one. It was so welcoming and meant so much to us.

Now, in the light of day, we stepped outside to look closer at the snow on the ground. We scooped up handfuls of snow, molding snowballs and feeling its cold and icy consistency. The snow in my hands was reminiscent of shaved ice cones with flavors and color that we ate as treats at special events when we were young. Channy and I chatted: *"Maybe we can eat the snow like we did those shaved ice cones so long ago?"* Glenda heard us as she peeked her head out the door and called out to us: *"Oh no! The snow's not for eating!"*

We began settling into our new home and our new lives with Glenda and her two cats: Kitty and Duke. Glenda suggested that Channy and I stay home, rest for a few days, and quietly adjust to our new surroundings while she went to work. A week later we were enrolled in an English as a Second Language (ESL) class and began our lessons. We already spoke English, but we worked on improving our language skills as well as our English reading and writing skills.

At the house Channy and I shared a bedroom with twin beds. I'd never slept in a room within a house that was enclosed by four walls. I had difficulty sleeping. Each night I'd grab my pillow and blanket and move out to the living room couch instead. I was uneasy and worried about our safety. I'd peer out the windows and double-check the locks. I suffered from disturbing nightmares, then I'd wake up screaming. I took a sharp knife from the kitchen drawer and kept it close by when sleeping.

We didn't receive medical insurance like others who immigrated with "refugee status." Our immigration status was as "humanitarian parolees (HP)." However, Glenda was dogged in seeking out medical insurance for us. Eventually, both of us were approved for and started receiving medical insurance. Once my insurance was in place, Glenda recommended that I be seen for a mental health evaluation. She could tell that I was struggling. I scheduled appointments with both a psychologist and a psychiatrist and began regular therapy sessions. I was diagnosed with post-traumatic stress disorder (PTSD), depression, and anxiety.

During these sessions I shared my story. I found the telling to be traumatizing and uncomfortable. I cried at each visit. I had a lot of work to do to begin healing from the psychological trauma that the prolonged wartime years had on my mental health. In therapy I learned a variety of techniques to foster relaxation in my daily life. Visual meditation I found to be an especially effective therapeutic practice for me. My therapist guided me in learning how to escape to a visual place in my mind that was serene and peaceful, to linger there while listening to soothing music. With my therapist's assistance, I came up with a mantra that I'd recite to myself at bedtime: *"Veera, you are in the United States now. No war is happening here. You are safe. Nothing will hurt you. Everybody will be fine. My family will be fine."* My favorite Cambodian music was too sad to listen to, so I didn't listen to it. At bedtime I listened to peaceful classical music instead. This process of working through my PTSD took many years of therapy.

In therapy we also addressed my issues of depression and anxiety. I learned that my feelings of sadness, loss of interest in doing things that had once provided me with pleasure, my tendency to cry easily, my poor appetite, my feelings of hopelessness, and my trust issues were all symptoms of depression. When I arrived in the US I didn't trust anybody, *especially* Cambodian people. Living in Khmer Rouge work camps ingrained in me that trusting others could actually be life-threatening. While living in the resettlement camps and finally the refugee camps, I feared that trusting others would jeopardize any opportunities I might have to make a better life for myself by immigrating to a third country. My trust wasn't easily earned. Both therapy and Glenda helped me to work through a lot of these unhealthy and self-protective walls I had up, and to eventually learn to live with less fear.

Glenda was instrumental in encouraging us to further our education. She researched which local colleges require no high school diploma or GED. Channy and I both took College Entry Assessment Exams and passed. We enrolled in a pre-nursing program at Minneapolis Community College (MCC). We learned to use public transportation and began commuting to and from college by bus. We attended morning classes. Our afternoons were spent in a work-study program in a childcare center. We completed the pre-nursing program in two years while also attending ESL classes.

We transferred to Inver Hills Community College and enrolled in the nursing program. Channy and I successfully got our driver's licenses before the beginning of the school year. I bought a used car, and we drove ourselves to college in a nearby suburb. Nursing school was challenging for both of us. The curriculum included classes in technology, microbiology, children's psychology, geriatric psychology, and others. Because the English language was still so new to me, the material was difficult to grasp. I studied very hard. Although I understood a lot, my anxiety made it difficult for me to concentrate in a large classroom setting where one hundred students took the final exam together. When students finished ahead of me, I got very anxious. I was unable to successfully pass my final exam.

After failing the first year of nursing school, I withdrew from the program. It was difficult to surrender this dream of mine to work in the nursing field, but repeating the program for a second year would be too much of a challenge for me both academically and financially. I remained at Inver Hills Community College and earned my associate degree in human services. Channy transferred to Metropolitan State University and went on to earn her associate degree in chemical dependency.

Another important undertaking was to apply for our Green Cards so that we could stay permanently in the United States. Glenda, our sponsor and advisor, was uncertain whether our case as humanitarian parolees would allow us to apply for a

Green Card (a Permanent Resident Card). At that time, all refugees who immigrated to the US from refugee camps were given an I-94 status and visas that designated how long one could remain in the US, but with our HP status the time period was left open-ended.

A physical exam was required. I learned that I'm a hepatitis B carrier. I have the HB (hepatitis B) virus in my blood. If left untreated, the HB virus would lead to inflammation of my liver. Fortunately, I had no symptoms. My earlier immigration physical didn't screen for hepatitis because those people with hepatitis were allowed to immigrate to the US. Because my mother died from a form of hepatitis, my doctor told me that I was likely genetically predisposed for it. No treatment was necessary, however semiannual ultrasounds to monitor my liver function were recommended. Years later, a liver specialist recommended that I take medication to suppress the hepatitis B virus in my blood. Over time the HBV virus has become undetectable in my blood. The drug suppresses but does not kill the hepatitis B virus, so I must remain on this medication indefinitely.

I received my Green Card and permanent residency in 1993, as did Channy. In August 1994, I became a US citizen.

My life was progressing well in America. I was actively pursuing my dreams and goals here in Minnesota. Channy and I successfully completed our college degrees and were qualified for professional employment. We'd both become US citizens, and now we set our sights on bringing our father and the rest of our family from Cambodia to the United States to live. I made phone calls to my family a few times each month and kept current on their daily health and financial struggles. My sister Sarem was very sick with hepatitis B. My family in Cambodia was struggling to make ends meet. Hearing of their struggles back in my home country was stressful. I was motivated to earn a better income so that I could afford to provide my family with more financial support.

In 1991, I started working at the United Cambodian Association of Minnesota (UCAM) earning a better salary. Channy was also hired by them. She picked up a second job at the MSP Airport washing dishes that were unloaded from airplanes. We were grateful and fortunate to continue to live with Glenda, especially because our sponsor was an immigration lawyer. She gave us so much assistance and guidance in our efforts to bring our extended family to the United States.

Our first family member to immigrate to the US and to Minnesota was our youngest sibling and brother, Rithea. He arrived here in July 1991. Glenda welcomed Rithea to live in her home along with the two of us. In fact, when we did decide to all move out of Glenda's home, she was very sad. Rithea began ESL classes and soon started working at the MSP Airport with Channy, washing dishes. Three months later, Channy, Rithea, and I moved out of Glenda's home and began renting an apartment in the West Seventh Street neighborhood in Saint Paul. In 1994, Channy and I purchased a house together in Eagan where the three of us siblings lived together.

I made a job change in 1995 and started working at the University of Minnesota Community Health Care Center (CUHCC) as a medical interpreter. (I continued this work for 24 years.) In 2014, Fairview University Medical Center took over the U of M

Community Health Care Center, and later, after one more transition, the center became known as M Health.

In 1995, I applied with Immigration to sponsor my father and my remaining four siblings and their families still living in Cambodia: Saly, Sarem, Navy, and Rithy. Our friend Paul, who illegally entered Khao I Dang Refugee Camp with us in 1986, had immigrated to the state of Washington. He paid us a visit to Minnesota about this time. Paul and Channy began a relationship and later became engaged to be married.

Due to the war in Cambodia starting in 1975 and my subsequent immigration to the US, I spent many years not able to see my dad. When he came to America, it was my intention to finally be able to take good care of him and to show him my deep gratitude for all he and my mother had done for me. We were so poor. Now, here I was successfully caring for myself and living and working in the United States of America. I couldn't have been more excited for my dad to get here.

My dad first arrived in Eagan in 1995. He was 70 years old and blind in one eye due to glaucoma. I was living with Channy and Rithea at that time, and our father stayed there with us. He received a Green Card that allowed him to remain in the US permanently. I was eager to take him here and there to see the sights and dine out at the local restaurants. My father had no interest in that. The only thing he was interested in doing was spending time at the temple. He did not speak English and wasn't fond of the Minnesota weather. He became restless here. Before long, he wanted to return to Cambodia to live. I worried about his health. He needed daily doses of medication for his glaucoma, and the medicine wasn't readily available in Cambodia. I encouraged him to stay here, and assured him that I would do whatever I could so that he could visit the temple every day if he stayed. *"Dad, you may not need me, but I need you,"* I told him. Dad had his mind made up to return to Cambodia in spite of his need for eye care. Two years after his arrival in Minnesota, he was living back home in Cambodia.

Paul and Channy traveled back to Cambodia to have their wedding and were married on May 10, 1998. Channy purchased my share of our home from me when she married Paul. I then purchased a town home in Eagan, and my brother Rithea and I moved in.

A few years later, in 2000, my father sponsored his wife, my stepmother, Touch Heng, to immigrate to the US. Dad was back in Minnesota again, but this time along with his wife. They moved in with Channy and family. I hoped my father and step-mom would remain here permanently, but this time my parents returned to Cambodia four years later. Dad was constantly homesick, the weather was a factor, and he said he did not want to die in Eagan. My father lived the remainder of his life in Cambodia. He lived to be 91 years old.

Back in 1997, when my father was still living in Eagan, my brother Rithy was a victim of a car accident in Cambodia and died. Because my brother, a blood relative, was now deceased, I was no longer allowed through Immigration to sponsor Rithy's wife, Sophann, and her daughters, Mealea and Molly, to immigrate to the US. Sophann, despite the fact I could no longer sponsor her to immigrate to the US, still wanted her two daughters to immigrate and have the opportunity for a good education and improved living conditions here in the United States. Given my brother Rithy's passing, the only way that I could still sponsor my two nieces was for me to adopt them. At Sophann's urging, I agreed to adopt each of the girls. We retained a lawyer in Cambodia. The girls' mother understood that once her daughters' adoptions were finalized and the girls became American citizens, that they would not be able to sponsor her immigration. As a result of the girls' adoption, Sophann would no longer be their legal parent. I would be. Despite knowing this, Sophann chose to proceed with my adoption of the girls and their subsequent immigration.

Veera's brother Rithy, father of Mealea and Molly. *Photo credit: Veera Som.*

Molly, Mealea and Sodon dancing at Minnesota Temple.
Photo credit: Donna May Sanders.

I worked with Children's Home Society of Minnesota to complete Mealea and Molly's designated adoptions. Once the adoption process and immigration arrangements were in place, Mealea (11) and Molly (6) immigrated to the United States. They both arrived in Minnesota together on Thursday, December 12, 2002. Mealea and Molly were now legally my daughters. I was now a first-time single mother, and Mealea and Molly were now American citizens.

Sadly, in 2001, the year before my daughters arrived, my sister Sarem lost her battle with hepatitis B and passed away. In 2004, I sponsored my sister Sarem's sons Sodan (10) and Sodon (6). They arrived in the United States in Eagan, Minnesota, on Thursday, March 18, 2004, and became American citizens.

Veera's sister, Sarem, mother of
Sodan and Sodon.
Photo credit: Veera Som.

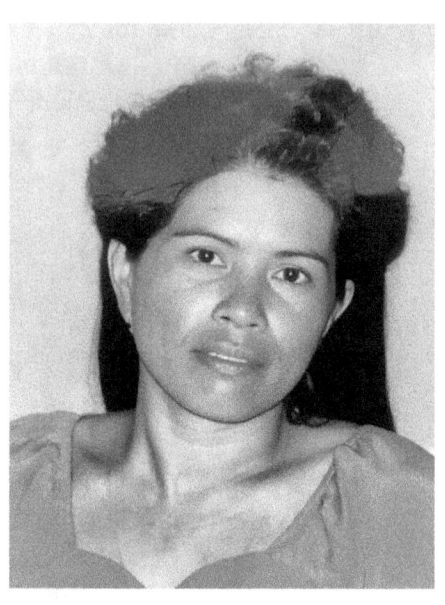

Veera and Family, Channy, Paul and Amelia, and Donna and Conrad on
Veera's deck, celebrating Sodan's high school graduation.
Photo credit: Donna May Sanders.

Veera's sons, (left) Sodon and (right) Sodan. *Photo credit: Veera Som.*

Veera with her family: Sodan, Sodon, Mealea, Molly and Eysan, taken at Veera's Eagan home. *Photo credit: Veera Som.*

I was now a single working mother raising four children. My two girls and two boys, who'd previously been cousins, were now living as brothers and sisters. We all had some adjusting to do, but because we'd always been extended family, it made it simpler. My kids attended public school. ESL classes were offered at their schools, which was very beneficial and convenient. I was a member of the Minnesota Temple (Watt Munisotaram), located in Hampton, MN, in Dakota County, since 1989. The temple had been built and established in 1988. It was located approximately 12 miles south of our home in Eagan. I was happy to raise my children in this Buddhist community with strong ties to our home culture.

Learning English was built into my children's school curriculum. Even though studies of their Cambodian culture and literature were not a part of their formal curriculum, these studies were a priority for me. No matter how tired I was at the end of my workday, I'd come home, cook dinner, then teach my children their lessons in Cambodian culture and literature.

Initially, when my four kids arrived, we were all living in my townhouse. I enrolled my children at Glacier Hills Elementary School located close to my sister Channy's home so they could take the school bus after school and be dropped off at her house with their grandparents or whoever was home at the time. They could remain there until I picked them up after work.

In 2005 I began planning for the arrival and immigration of two more of my sisters and their families to the US. With this in mind, in December 2005 I purchased another home, this one larger than my townhouse with five bedrooms and three baths also in Eagan. I kept my townhouse and rented it out.

In 2007 my sister Navy, her husband Kim Chhoun, and their four children—Pisith Lim, Kanika Lim, Pekadey Lim, and Chhoung Lim—all immigrated from Cambodia. Most of their family moved in with Channy and Paul, and a few of the adult children stayed with Glenda temporarily. When my renters' lease expired, Navy and family moved into my townhouse.

Navy and family at Minnesota Temple. *Photo credit: Veera Som.*

Later that same year, 2007, my sister Saly, her husband Sare-oung, and their adult children Marina, Raya, and Reksa (now Rita) immigrated from Cambodia. They moved into my Eagan home with me and my family. Saly's son, Sarak Korng, remained in Cambodia because he was ineligible for immigration, as he was older than 21 years of age. Marina's young son, Meng Heng, stayed behind. Years later Meng Heng joined his mother in America.

Veera's extended family photo Saly and Family, Sokmen, and others. *Photo credit: Veera Som.*

At this point in time, my father, my stepmother, and all of my living siblings and their children, had immigrated to the United States (with the exception of Saly's son Sarak and Marina's son Meng Heang).

Sponsoring people wishing to immigrate to America is no simple task. The US has strict sponsorship regulations. For the immigrants, the sponsor must take responsibility for their food, shelter, transportation, education arrangements, job searches, and support them in the process of getting their driver's licenses, and more. There was much to do. Despite all of that, I was delighted to have my family here in the United States and in

Minnesota with me. My sister Channy and I had achieved this significant, challenging, and rewarding goal to bring our family to the US to live.

Reunion with ARC friends at Glenda's home: Jeff Nelson with glasses, Jean Jachman in 2nd row third from right, Veera in back, Monica Overkamp next to Veera, Glenda Potter, Immigration Lawyer.
Photo credit: Veera Som.

In late 2006, my friend, sponsor, and angel, Glenda Potter, was diagnosed with stage 5 breast cancer. The cancer had already metastasized throughout her body, specifically to her leg and her spinal cord. I was heartbroken. Glenda had done so much for me and my family. It was now our turn to give back to her. She had chemotherapy and tolerated it well. We served her in any way that we could. When her condition became debilitating, my family and I looked after Glenda and provided for all of her personal care needs. At the end of her life her parents and sister were making plans for hospice care. We met and I assured them that my family and I could care for Glenda in her home. Her mother said, *"But Veera, you're so tiny, how can you provide her care?"* I told her: *"I may be small, but my heart is not."* My family, friends and I scheduled ourselves around the clock to care for her. It was an honor.

Glenda touched many lives in her work in immigration, especially in the Cambodian community. We organized a fundraiser for her at the United Cambodian Association of Minnesota (UCAM) to raise funds for her health care needs. We surpassed our expectations, raising tens of thousands of dollars.

Glenda's precious cat, Duke, cuddled with her day and night. Just before she was about to leave us on January 3, 2011, Duke screeched in warning, and then Glenda was gone. The next morning her family made plans to transport her to Farmington for her burial. Glenda's Cambodian family and I cried. We didn't want them to take her away before we could pay our final respects to her. Glenda's family had no idea that she was so beloved by the Cambodian community. So instead, her family selected a church more centrally located in Minneapolis. An estimated 500 people gathered to pay their respects to Glenda. The fundraising money easily covered Glenda's funeral expenses.

I'm proud of what my family has accomplished since immigrating to the United States and becoming legal American citizens. We are self-driven, work steady jobs, and our children each earned a quality education. We purchased our own homes and vehicles. We credit our success in obtaining the "American dream" to our parents who raised strong children that are independent and patient. Our father believed that women need not be dependent on men to be successful, and that women can be equal partners, as my parents were. My four children each grad-uated from high school and are pursuing their independent lives away from home.

In 2014, I agreed to sponsor a young woman, Eysan Kloeng, who had won an immigration lottery in Cambodia. What's in-volved with such a sponsorship? In Cambodia, non-family mem-bers of American citizens enter a lottery system for eligibility to immigrate to the US. But first, they need to identify a US citizen willing to sponsor them. I made the commitment to Eysan before having met her, and invited her to live with me in my home. We've become close and share a familial bond. Our relationship is now that of mother and daughter. In 2021 Eysan returned to Cambodia to marry Makra Pen, her betrothed. They currently re-side in Eagan, Minnesota with their daughter Sanathara.

Veera with daughter Eysan, at Minnesota Temple. *Photo credit: Veera Som.*

Veera with daughters Mealea and Eysan. *Photo credit: Veera Som.*

In 2017, while on a pilgrimage in Sri Lanka, I met Sokmen Yem, a young Cambodian monk who was living and studying in Sri Lanka. Later in 2019 on a climb to the summit of an historic ruin, I struggled to continue the climb and Sokmen, who was nearby, stepped in and assisted me the rest of the way. We soon became well acquainted. As a child Sokmen lost his mother. His father remains in Cambodia. A familial bond, that of a mother and son, grew between us. We kept in touch, with Sokmen living in Sri Lanka and me living in Eagan. I've had the privilege of assisting Sokmen with financial support for his continued education and academic pursuits. In 2022, my son Sokmen arrived in Minnesota. He lives, works, and studies as a monk at the Minnesota Temple.

Sokmen and Veera sitting at Minnesota Temple.
Photo credit: Veera Som.

Eysan and husband Makra; Veera, and Sokmen.
Photo credit: Veera Som.

As an empty nester, I spent much of my time at the temple volunteering and studying Buddhism at home. I have traveled extensively, both domestically and internationally, with my temple community, as well as visiting family. I joined monks and devotees from my temple on pilgrimages to India, Sri Lanka, and Burma, all of these locations on more than one occasion. I participated in a pilgrimage to Nepal, the birthplace of Buddha. We visited sites of historic significance of the Buddha. I have returned to Cambodia for visits multiple times since 1989, when I left there. I've traveled to Vietnam three times. Some of these travels have taken place since retiring in January 2019, following my twenty-four-year career as a medical interpreter.

Raya and Veera at Preah
Sihanouk Raja Buddhist
University, Cambodia.
Photo credit: Veera Som.

Veera presented with
certificate at Preah
Sihanouk Raja
Buddhist University,
Cambodia.
Photo credit: Veera Som.

Veera at writing desk at Meditation Center, Cambodia.
Photo credit: Veera Som.

Philanthropy

Veera is a philanthropist who's given back to her community both here in the US, and abroad. She has awarded scholarships for one bachelor's degree; six two-year master's degrees, and one three-year PhD degree in philosophy and Buddhism to monks and a nun; she's provided a business start-up loan for an entrepreneur in Minnesota; made a much-needed food donation for 30 poor families in her hometown village; and, knowing the lack of opportunities a farm girl like her had growing up in Cambodia, Veera paid for another poor farm girl's tuition to medical school. This woman is currently an M.D. in Cambodia, thanks in part to Veera.

Conclusion

Veera and Living Siblings: top to bottom step: Veera, Saly, Channy, Navy and Rithea.
Photo credit: Veera Som.

My surviving siblings and I are American citizens. Minnesota was our first home in the US, now we have family members in the midwest in Minnesota, south in Mississippi and Florida, and southwest in New Mexico. I am proud and extremely grateful for what my family and I have achieved here in the United States. We came from meager beginnings in northwestern Cambodia and were raised by poor peasant farmers. We endured the ravages of a civil war and lived through the Cambodian Genocide. Every struggle that I've experienced on my life's journey has molded and shaped me into the strong individual that I am today. I believe the suffering and misery that I've endured throughout my journey is karma from a past life, that I have carried and have atoned for.

A Buddhist Reflection on War, Suffering, and the Path to Peace
~Ven. Sokmen Yem

The journey described in these chapters of growing up in Cambodia, enduring the brutality of the Khmer Rouge, and finally resettling in the United States reveals profound truths about the nature of suffering (dukkha), impermanence (anicca), and the roots of human conflict. Through a Buddhist lens, these painful experiences are not just personal tragedies, but reflections of deeper truths the Buddha taught over 2,500 years ago.

Kamma and the Causes of War

From the Buddhist perspective, the law of *Kamma* (karma) explains that all intentional actions whether of body, speech, or mind bear fruit. War, violence, and mass suffering do not arise randomly; they are the karmic results of collective greed, hatred, and ignorance built up over time. When leaders or societies act out of selfish desire (*lobha*), anger (*dosa*), or delusion (*moha*), they plant seeds of future suffering. People are drawn into war due to the karmic momentum of past actions and mental habits. A nation shaped by unwholesome deeds will, without correction, repeat cycles of violence. Only through conscious ethical action through generosity, compassion, and wisdom can we break this cycle and prevent war's return.

In the Pali Canon, the Buddha explained that *tanha*, or craving, lies at the root of suffering. The desire for power, control, recognition, or vengeance fuels the unwholesome actions of individuals and governments. The Khmer Rouge, driven by ideology and hatred, sought to reshape society through violence and fear. This craving for a utopian vision led to the destruction of lives, culture, and families. As seen in the killing fields and the forced labor camps, the delusion (*moha*) of leaders combined with greed (*lobha*) and hatred (*dosa*) becomes the triple poison that drives mass suffering.

The Cambodian genocide illustrates what happens when these poisons go unchecked how fear and attachment to false views can dehumanize others. Those labeled enemies were killed not for their actions, but for their identity or perceived threat. As the Buddha taught in the *Dhammapada*:

> *Hatred is never appeased by hatred in this world. By non-hatred alone is hatred appeased. This is an eternal law.*
> ~Dhammapada, verse 5

From the perspective of Dharma, even those who commit grave harm are not beyond the reach of compassion. The teachings remind us that every being carries seeds of both delusion and awakening. Forgiveness, then, is not forgetting or condoning the past, but a deliberate turning of the heart away from vengeance. It is the release of suffering, the abandoning of anger, so that healing may begin.

Those who survived like the narrator of this memoir show us the strength of *kshanti* (patience) and *mettā* (loving-kindness). Despite the loss of loved ones, illness, and trauma, the author chose to work in healthcare, to relieve the suffering of others, to protect life instead of taking it. This is *right action (sammā-kammanta)* in the Eightfold Path.

Ultimately, the path to peace is not found through political ideologies or armies, but through inner transformation. As long as greed, hatred, and delusion dominate the minds of individuals, conflict will continue. But through mindfulness, ethical living, and compassion, even a single person can become a light in the darkness. The peace the world seeks begins in the heart.

Let the suffering of the past remind us: impermanence spares no one. What is born will die, what is built will fall. But peace true peace arises when we let go, when we forgive, and when we choose love over fear.

In the words of the Buddha:

"Just as a solid rock is not shaken by the storm, even so the wise are not affected by praise or blame." (*Dhammapada*, verse 81)

May all beings be free from suffering. May all find peace.

Veera picking watergrass. *Photo credit: Veera Som.*

Sokrey and Veera.
Photo credit: Sokrey.

Sokrey's parents planting Asian basil. *Photo credit: Sokrey.*

Extended family Channy and Paul; Veera, Sokmen, Sodan; Saly and Family, and Navy and Family. *Photo credit: Veera Som.*

Channy, Venerable Moeng Sang, Abbot of MN Temple, Veera, and Theavy, Secretary, Minnesota Temple. *Photo credit: Veera Som.*

Paul and daughter, Amelia (Channy's husband) *Photo credit: Veera Som.*

Channy and daughter, Amelia (Channy's husband) *Photo credit: Veera Som.*

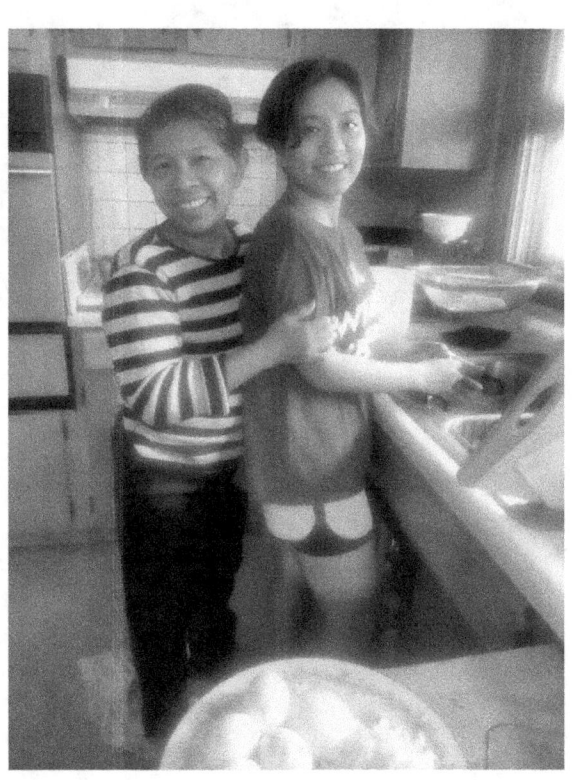

Veera returns to Cambodia for a visit. Picking yellow flowers.
Photo credit: Veera Som.

Further Exploration: Additional Titles on the Cambodian Genocide

Hood, Doug. *Daughter of Song: A Cambodian Refugee Family, Their Daughter, Crime, and Injustice.* Foreword by Wally Lamb. Atacama Books, LLC, 2022.

Laux, Channy Chhi. *Short Hair Detention.* Archway Publishing, 2017.

Charles River Editors. *The Khmer Rouge: The Notorious History and Legacy of the Communist Regime that Ruled Cambodia in the 1970s.* Charles River Editors, 2018.

Lei, Sida Kong, with Monica Boothe. *Two Teaspoons of Rice: A Memoir of a Cambodian Orphan.* Blue Ridge Software Consulting, 2020.

Ngor, Haing S., with Roger Warner. *Survival in the Killing Fields.* New York: Basic Books (Carroll & Graf Publishers), 2003.

Pilch, Frances T. *Invisible: Surviving the Cambodian Genocide: The Memoirs of Mac and Simone Leng.* Bandon, OR: Robert D. Reed Publishers, 2017.

Seng, Seang M., MD. *Starving Season: One Person's Story.* Morrisville, NC: Lulu Publishing Services, 2017.

Schanberg, Sydney H. *The Death and Life of Dith Pran.* New York: Penguin Books, 1985.

Ty, Seng. *The Years of Zero: Coming of Age Under the Khmer Rouge.* Morrisville, NC: CreateSpace Independent Publishing Platform, 2014.

Ung, Loung. *First They Killed My Father: A Daughter of Cambodia Remembers.* New York: HarperCollins Publishers, 2000.

www.ingramcontent.com/pod-product-compliance
Lightning Source LLC
Chambersburg PA
CBHW071354120626
46546CB00002B/686